TITANIUM

TITANIUM

EMBRACING THE STRENGTH WITHIN TO OVERCOME LIFE'S CHALLENGES

LORI BARBAROTTO

SB
PRESS

CONTENTS

To my father—a man I have always
admired and learned so much from.

You showed me the value of hard work,
perseverance, creativity, and love.

Even as you faced the challenges of ALS,
your strength and spirit never wavered.

Your legacy lives on in me and in
every page of this book.

CHAPTER 1

THE POWER OF INNER TITANIUM

It was June 24th, 2011—a summer day that began like any other with my usual 4:30 a.m. workout at the local park. I was in a very healthy stage of my life at the time, and I'd met my daily workout partner there, a friend who lived a mile away. We completed our circuit of running the hill at the park, sprints, and burpees. This was always a good way to kick off my Friday morning as I moved into the fun active weekends with the kids and husband. We wrapped up around 5:30 a.m., and I hopped in my car to head home, a simple mile drive.

On many days, our master planned community reminded me of a scene straight out of *The Stepford Wives*. There was a constant hum of activity—young, growing families settling into their brand-new homes, each with perfectly maintained desert landscaping and spotless driveways. The streets were mostly clear—no street parking was the rule—but every now and then, you'd spot a lone car parked neatly along the curb, like it had permission to be there. The community center had it all: swimming lessons, soccer leagues, story time, yoga classes. It was a safe little bubble, and we all lived in it together.

But let's be clear—this wasn't some scripted fantasy. Behind the manicured rock gardens and quiet sidewalks were strong, amazing women. Many had loving, supportive spouses, and the friendships I formed during that time were some of the most genuine and lasting I've ever known. I continue to cherish them to this day.

As I pulled into my driveway that morning, exhausted and ready to start the day, I had no idea I was about to be thrust into a nightmare. There was no warning, no eerie music in the background, just the usual rhythm of suburban calm. But within moments, I was about to be pulled into something I couldn't have prepared for—an event that would shake me, change me, and force me to see the world through entirely different eyes.

WHERE TERROR TOOK ME

The sound of my car's engine idling was the only noise as I pulled into my driveway and parked, about to step out and head inside to get ready for work. This Friday was payday, and all was going wonderfully for me and the family. But as I reached for the handle to open my door to exit my car, my safe little bubble burst.

A sudden movement caught my eye. Before I could react, a masked man appeared in front of me, his face hidden behind a dark bandana only revealing his eyes and dark glasses. My heart slammed into my chest as I froze, unable to comprehend what was happening. He was so close—too close—and then I saw it: the cold steel of a gun, pressed firmly against my chest.

"Get back in the car," he ordered, his voice low and menacing.

I didn't have a choice. Every part of me screamed to run, but fear paralyzed me. After giving a quick gasp and loud squeal, I slowly slid back into the driver's seat.

"Unlock the back," he commanded, his tone sharp. With trembling fingers, I clicked the button, unlocking the back doors. The man climbed in. His presence and the thought of the gun pressed against my ribs as I froze was suffocating.

I remember I did as he asked. He settled directly behind me. I could feel his eyes on me, even though I never saw his face. The gun was still there, aimed at my back.

"Backout of your driveway and drive," he said, his voice colder now, almost a whisper.

I shifted into reverse, hands still trembling on the steering wheel, and slowly backed out.

I didn't know where we were going or what would happen next. My mind raced, adrenaline flooding my system, but all I could do was to make sure I followed his orders. I had no idea what kind of hell was about to unfold.

Time seemed to slow down, and I found myself unable to think, yet every detail felt oddly vivid. Meanwhile, my daughter, who was about ten years old at the time, had been in her room above the driveway, directly overlooking the scene. She always watched for me when I arrived home, her bed positioned by the front window. That morning she had just been woken up by my husband to get ready to start her day at summer camp. As she heard my voice outside, she peeked through the curtains and saw the masked man standing there with the gun pointed at me. Everything happened so quickly.

In a panic as we started to back out of the driveway, she rushed into our bedroom where my husband was getting ready for work, urgently telling him, "Mom's getting robbed." He was stunned, thinking she was still groggy from a bad dream. She ran down the front stairs to our entrance way, and when they opened the front door to look out, I was already gone.

Meanwhile, as I sat in the car with the man still holding the gun pointed at my back, I noticed a white Nissan Altima following us. Another man was driving, tailing us a few feet behind. I could see my phone vibrating alongside me—calls from my husband—but I couldn't answer. The kidnapper had ordered me to drive to my bank, and it felt like my mind was on autopilot, some voice deep inside me guiding my every move.

Back at the house, my husband—an experienced gun owner—had already grabbed his weapon from the safe. He was still in shock, trying to make sense of what our daughter had just told him. Part of him questioned whether it could really be true. Maybe she'd misunderstood. Maybe she was still half-asleep. But something in her voice—urgent, terrified— pushed him to act.

Before running out the door, he ordered her to stay inside and make sure the door was locked.

"Don't open it for anyone," he told her firmly. She nodded, wide-eyed, and he left, not knowing what he was heading into.

He assumed I couldn't have gone far. Thinking I might be headed toward the sheriff's station, he jumped into his car and turned left onto Main Street.

But in reality, we had gone the opposite way.

It still chills me to think what might have happened if he had chosen differently—if he had turned right instead of left and caught up to us. He was armed. The man behind me was armed. Both would have been on edge, adrenaline high, hearts pounding. One wrong move, one instinctive reaction, and everything could've spiraled into chaos—a standoff, a misfire, a loss none of us would have recovered from.

That one left turn made in uncertainty may have been what saved us all.

As my husband continued searching for me and later contacting the authorities, I was being directed to a well-known bank ATM drive-thru. The man ordered me to withdraw the maximum amount of money. The timing couldn't have been more critical; I had just been paid, and our checking account at that time had a substantial balance to pay our mortgage. I was acutely aware of the surveillance cameras recording me, recognizing this ATM as one I used often. I hoped someone, somewhere, would notice something was off.

When he saw how low my daily withdrawal limit was, his tone shifted. He told me to grab my phone and call the bank—using the number on the back of my ATM card—to request an increase to the limit. That's when it truly hit me: this wasn't random. It was calculated. He had a plan.

I remember forcing myself to sound calm, like I was simply handling an everyday banking issue. My voice steady, my tone casual, even as my heart raced. I navigated the phone tree quickly, thankful I knew the system well, and was soon connected to a live representative.

In that moment, I knew—if I slipped, even a little, if I gave the slightest sign that something was wrong—it could all go sideways. I had no choice. I had to keep my cool.

I remember fumbling to originally make the call, and he threatened me not to do anything sneaky. I made the call in a trance that took over, guiding me through the steps quickly. After calling the bank to raise my limit, I completed several individual withdrawals, taking out just under $3000 and leaving a small balance.

But my mind wasn't on the money—not anymore. It was on leaving a trail. Evidence. Anything that could help identify this man if things went terribly wrong.

Instincts I hadn't used in years suddenly surged forward. Before moving to Arizona, I had dreamed of going into law enforcement. And before that, I'd spent years in loss prevention, catching shoplifters in the streets and department stores of San Francisco. Those experiences, long buried beneath the layers of daily life and motherhood, came rushing back.

In that moment, I became the tough, sharp version of myself I hadn't seen in a long time—the one who stayed composed under pressure, who read body language, who thought two steps ahead—just when I needed her most.

As I handed him the money after each transaction, I deliberately positioned myself so the ATM camera had a clear view—not only of the exchange, but of his hands reaching out and, if possible, a glimpse of his face from the camera's angle. I moved with intention, calculating every small adjustment, hoping each gesture would be recorded. My mind was racing, trying to capture every detail—his hand size, any markings, the texture of his skin, even the presence of hair on his hands. I was grasping at whatever I could observe. He wore gloves, so all I could make out were the size of his hands and his body hair, but I took it all in.

He then told me to open my cell phone and remove my battery and give them both to him. In that instant, I was completely cut off—no way to connect with anyone, no way for anyone to track my phone and find me. I was utterly vulnerable.

At one point, his dark bandana slipped off his nose and face, briefly exposing his round face. I saw it for a split second before he quickly adjusted it back into place, unsure if he realized I had seen his face in the rearview mirror. Despite the chaos, I forced myself to stay composed and asked him quietly, "Will you let me go?"

He responded, "As long as you don't pull anything, but we'll see about that as you got a little crazy at first." I realized then he had no intention of letting me go.

As we exited the ATM drive-thru, I saw two possible routes from the bank: one passed through a gas station parking lot with cameras to exit to the main road, and the other, a quick right turn that led to the main highway, close to the entrance to our community. I remained calm, though a gnawing fear crept in—this felt like it could be the end. Kidnappings weren't unheard of in parts of Arizona, and the reality of what was happening began to settle in.

I deliberately started to go to the camera route in front of the store. I also made a point to drive slow, passing the gas station, hoping the surveillance camera might capture something that could later help. As he ordered me to turn left, away from the highway and into a quieter section of our community, the stark contrast of our surroundings hit me. Our neighborhood, with its pristine streets and families always out walking their dogs, felt like the last place something like this should happen. It was the kind of place where crime was rare, and yet, here I was—trapped with a man holding a gun, unsure of what would come next in the very early hours of the morning as the roads still remained stark and quiet.

As we drove, the man directed me toward an open field on the outskirts of our community. It was apparent he was very familiar with our community. I knew this construction area well; it was the site where they planned to build a new church in the future. But right now it seemed like a desolate, empty place, one that filled me with dread. My heart pounded in my chest as I wondered if this was where they would leave me to die—or worse. The field stretched out ahead, quiet and barren, as if it was waiting for something terrible to happen.

I couldn't shake the thought that this would be the end. My mind raced, spiraling into dark possibilities. Would I never see my family again? Would I be buried in the dirt, lost to the world? What was his plan? The terror surged, but I forced myself to stay visibly untroubled, hoping somehow, I could find a way out before it was too late.

Eventually, he directed me to one of the neighborhoods alongside the open construction, and we went in circles. As we drove past homes, I hoped a car would pass us or someone would see me driving, but it was quiet. I remember going in circles before he told me to stop in front of the community mailboxes. His phone rang, and he spoke briefly with someone on the other end. I had no idea what was coming. He ordered me to turn off the car, step out, and face the community mailboxes without looking back.

I remained eerily still. His threats were sharp before I exited the vehicle, ordering me not to tell anyone about the encounter, because he knew where I lived, and he'd come back to kill me if I did. He told me to count up to five minutes and not turn around until he was gone. I agreed. I was numb, almost in a trance, like I was outside of my own body looking at my calmness. He also exited my vehicle, but I was careful to not make any contact visually. I was giving him time to leave.

Time slowed to a crawl as I stood there, staring at the mailboxes, counting, feeling like I was stuck in a bad dream. When I caught a glimpse of the car he had gotten into turning onto a main street, I quickly tried to memorize the license plate. The trance broke, and panic surged through me. I screamed, desperate to release all the fear that had been building up inside. But it was the early hours of the morning, and no one came to help.

I continued reciting the license plate number as I hurried into my car, grabbed my keys, and sped home. Each mile felt like a lifetime, my mind flooded with thoughts as I tried to keep myself grounded until I could make it back to my family.

When I arrived, I found my husband with the garage door open. He ran out to me, looking concerned. I was shaken, unhinged, unsure how I had survived or how this had even happened. I was hysterical, my once tough little "muscles"—a nickname my dad always called me as a child for my strength— felt completely hollow, like the air had been sucked out of me, leaving behind a crushing wave of exhaustion.

My home was soon filled with sheriffs, detectives, and fingerprint specialists, all focused on the investigation into my kidnapping. They conducted intense interviews with my husband and daughter, trying to piece together what had happened. The aftermath was overwhelming. Local news outlets reported the story, and social media exploded with speculation, many people questioning my experience as unheard of in our bubble. Some were supportive, and some made assumptions and spread ridiculous rumors. It felt like the world had turned on me based on a few social media posts, so I chose to remove myself from following any more.

Working with a sketch artist to recall the kidnapper's features was a painful reminder of how much I had blocked out. I could only remember his glasses and face shape, and it was so hard to try to remember the view when his bandana fell for a few seconds. The sketches weren't fully accurate, and I grew frustrated, knowing I couldn't give them what they needed.

In the days that followed, fear consumed me. How could I leave the house? Were they watching, waiting to come back for me? Why did this happen? Why did I let my guard down on awareness? I had always prided myself on being strong, but now I felt vulnerable, living in a community I once thought was safe. I couldn't bring myself to speak to the news or show my face in public for fear he was waiting for me. I just wanted to disappear, especially since the trauma had happened in my own driveway, in front of my actual home.

As I shut down emotionally, I struggled to find my footing. My usual strength felt like it had slipped away. But the support of my community was a lifeline. They surrounded my family with meals, messages, and love, reminding me I wasn't alone. I soon realized after a few weeks that I was just another case for the sheriff's department. I wasn't the only one this had happened to recently, and although I'd had a much better outcome than some, no new leads emerged, and the photo lineup didn't yield anything. What seemed like just another cold case started to take shape. The authorities lacked the resources to pursue it further, and while they identified someone in the ATM footage in my back seat, it led to nothing.

I didn't have the energy to fight for answers; I just needed to heal.

Therapy became a part of our lives. My daughter and I saw a wonderful therapist, Amy, but my husband kept his emotions locked away and took on my usual role as the glue holding everything together. My son, still too young to understand, sensed the tension in our home as I learned from him many years later. Many days and nights I retreated to my room away from everyone to cry in private. My strength had turned to dust, and I felt utterly broken.

Healing was slow and painful. The thought of driving again filled me with panic. I was numb at the sight of any man wearing a bandana, which was very common for many on motorcycles in Arizona. I was convinced everyone around me was a threat and that *he* was somewhere lurking around every corner. But I had to find the strength to keep going for my family. I was their rock, and I refused to let this trauma define me. I didn't want any more attention or sympathy; I just wanted to pull myself together and find a way to move forward.

THE STRENGTH TO HEAL

A month or so after the kidnapping, I began driving again, just small trips to run errands or go to the store and back to work. Anything to ease myself back into a normal routine. On one of these trips, I was in my car when the David Guetta and Sia song "Titanium" came on the radio. It was one of those moments when everything clicked. The lyrics, "You shoot me down, but I won't fall / I am Titanium," spoke to me on the deepest levels, and this phrase became my internal mantra. But I also realized the concept of titanium described what I'd felt on June 24th. The calmness that had washed over me wasn't a relaxing feeling per se. It felt like an internal strength; a spirit of titanium. In hearing that song, this strength again welled up inside of me, and I knew I would come out of this.

I've always been someone who tends to internalize my thoughts. Whether it was through self-talk or divine guidance, this nightmare experience, and the song, solidified something I've always known: there is strength and direction beyond what we can see.

People hold a wide range of beliefs, whether rooted in religion, spirituality, or a secular worldview, and many would say this inner strength and direction was a connection to a higher power or purpose. For me, during this particular moment, it felt like something beyond the presence of a general sense of a higher power. It felt specific to me. The best way I can describe it is something like a guardian angel or a loved one who had passed sitting beside me, something or someone connected to me, guiding me through my journey. On the morning of the kidnapping, it was the voice in my head telling me to stay composed when a gun was pointed at me, helping me to think clearly about leaving a trail of evidence and memorizing the license plate. Afterwards, it became the strength to heal.

It was amazing how a song could give me strength and boost my confidence, but soon after, I started living that confidence, which made all of the difference. Those lyrics helped me in my journey to heal and, in doing so, made me reflect on my past journey. The song seemed to pop on when I needed to hear it most. I realized I had always relied on self-talk (again, divinely guided or otherwise) to boost my resilience. However, the true shift came when I made intentional changes in how I healed.

BECOMING STRONGER THAN BEFORE

Struggles take many shapes, often arriving when we least expect them. They can come in the form of heartbreaking loss, family or relationship turmoil, the quiet weight of self-doubt, the relentless pressure of work, or the lasting imprint of trauma. Sometimes they're loud and chaotic, other times they're silent and isolating—but no matter the form, they test us. They challenge our strength, shake our confidence, and force us to confront parts of ourselves we might not be ready to face. Yet within these struggles, we often discover what we're truly made of.

When we face these challenges, it's common to avoid sharing what we're going through. We don't want to feel vulnerable or seem weak or "burden" other people with our problems. However, there is a better way—a path that leads to growth, healing, and strength. That's where Titanium Strength comes in. Titanium is a symbol of strength and resilience, known for its remarkable ability to withstand pressure and adversity. But it's also malleable, so it can be shaped into different forms without breaking. This powerful metaphor reflects our own journeys: Like titanium, we too have the capacity to face challenges and emerge stronger than before—through embracing our personal strength, emotional malleability, and community.

For a long time, I kept my struggles to myself, thinking that staying silent and carrying the weight alone made me strong. But inner strength doesn't always come solely from within. It often comes from the people around us, even though it can be hard to lean on them. Recognizing and accepting that support—especially when it feels difficult—can be one of the most crucial, yet challenging, parts of healing. Sharing my burden with others sooner could have made the journey much easier.

Letting go, or being emotionally flexible, can be a transformative act. It often means releasing fears, doubts, and past experiences that no longer serve us. By learning to let go, we make room for empowerment and new possibilities, bringing greater clarity and purpose into our lives.

Community plays a vital role in this process. When we surround ourselves with supportive individuals, we strengthen our resolve and find encouragement during tough times. Together, we can uplift one another, celebrate our victories, and build resilience. If you don't yet have a community, know that it's possible to find one. I, too, had to search and expand mine. I found my community in unexpected places—whether through meaningful conversations, shared experiences, or by simply being open to new connections. Sometimes, finding the right people means stepping outside your comfort zone or seeking spaces where support and compassion thrive. By embracing our inner Titanium Strength, we can release what holds us back, tap into our power, and thrive with the support of those around us.

During challenging times, it's easy to feel lost or overwhelmed, but there is always a way forward. Finding that path required me to dig deep and discover a strength within myself I didn't know I had. If I wanted to return to being an independent person and an even stronger version than before, for myself and my family, I had to push through the fear.

MOVING FORWARD

My hope as you continue reading is that you'll begin to recognize the incredible strength within yourself because it's always been there, even in your darkest, most difficult moments. Maybe you've been the one who carries it all silently, internalizing your fears, your doubts, your trauma—unsure of who to turn to or how to speak the words out loud. But when you learn to tap into that inner power, something shifts. Healing begins. And with it, the ability to rise—not only for yourself, but for others, emerges. You'll find the courage to show up fully, to lead with compassion, and to lift those who are still trying to find their way through the dark.

CHAPTER 2

WHEN LIFE TESTS YOUR STRENGTH

Returning home felt like being hit by a tidal wave—crashing, overwhelming, and all-consuming. The day after the kidnapping, the events replayed in my mind, as if frozen in time—every detail, every moment, unfolding in slow motion: the feel of my husband's arms around me as I walked into the garage, the law enforcement officers filling my kitchen, the never-ending stream of questioning and interviews, feeling paralyzed, too numb to process the chaos unfolding around me. It felt like a nightmare I couldn't wake up from. The calm, peaceful life I had once taken for granted was gone, replaced by an avalanche of emotions and a deep, gnawing dread. All I could focus on was the suffocating fear for my family's safety.

The truth was this wasn't a random act. It was carefully planned. Someone had been watching me, studying my every move. My once predictable routine—morning trips to the gym or the park, Fridays at the ATM before work—had become a roadmap for someone intent on exploiting it. Every detail had been orchestrated, right down to the phone call I made to the bank at 6 a.m. to request an ATM limit increase. I had never noticed, never suspected, but someone had been tracking me. They had thought of everything. And in my attempt to embrace the peace of a new life in the desert, I had let my guard down. How wrong I was.

ROOTED AND RAISED IN THE CITY

I was born and raised in the Ingleside district of 1980s San Francisco, a city I've always considered beautiful, vibrant, and full of character. Life then was different— it was the era of latchkey kids. My parents worked tirelessly to support our family. My father was a San Francisco firefighter and worked as a cement mason on his days off while my mother balanced a career as a banker with raising two daughters and keeping a spotless home. Many years later, I understood their hard work provided those little extra things that gave me a wealth of experiences I later appreciated.

We were a middle-class family living on a budget, but we always had what mattered—a roof over our heads, food on the table, clothes to wear, and enough to cover tuition and uniforms so my sister and I could attend the local Catholic school. We were fortunate to have countless summers at our family cabin, tucked beneath the towering redwoods of Rio Nido, California, on the banks of Russian River. The cabin became a place of comfort, connection, experiences, and memory. Those summers weren't simply a tradition—they became part of our identity, cherished by both our family and the community we grew up in. We were surrounded by hardworking, supportive parents and grandparents who also lived in the city, as well as a close-knit family in a neighboring city that had each other's backs. It was a life of balance, sacrifice, and love all in the name of making sure we were cared for and could succeed.

Because of our parents' demanding schedules working to provide for us, my older sister Lisa and

I had a strong sense of independence and street-smarts. It was a time when kids were expected and able to look after themselves for a few hours when needed. Lisa and I knew the rules set by mom and dad and followed them for the most part as young teens, occasionally testing the waters. I looked up to Lisa, who was five years older than me, and wanted to be just like her: strong, smart, witty, the hilarious life of the party. Following her example, I quickly became street-smart and learned to stay aware of my surroundings from a young age. My sister and I could walk to school, bike around the neighborhood, even in tough areas, on our own. Without cell phones, we relied on house landlines and phone books, remembering the numbers we needed.

Being the youngest in my family, I was often the "runt"—or as my family and close friends lovingly called me, the TSEP (Pest spelled backward). I was always eager to be around the older kids, watching them, learning from them. In doing so, I learned early on that survival required toughness—both physical and mental.

It's something I deeply respect about myself. I wasn't pampered or shielded from the world; instead, I was taught to protect myself, to be a protector for others, and to lead. These values stayed with me, shaping who I've become as I approach five decades of life. From childhood on, I've always been there to defend my friends or anyone whom I felt was being treated unfairly, and today, that role of protector is just a more mature version of what it was back then.

I took my first job at the age of sixteen working in the "employee cage" of a well-known department store. I was responsible for greeting and checking employees' bags in and out as they began and ended their shifts. I was outgoing and very much a "by the book" kind of person, so I got to know everyone well, and I always followed the rules.

Sitting in the cage, I had access to the store's surveillance cameras, allowing me to monitor high-end departments where the Loss Prevention Team focused on catching shoplifters. I had a natural talent for spotting them. Before long, I was promoted to a store detective position. From there, I soon climbed the ranks to become the manager of Loss Prevention and eventually, a Region Internal Investigator for the same large retail chain.

Growing up surrounded by firefighters and police officers, I always felt a strong calling to serve and protect, which naturally led me toward a career in law enforcement. In my new role as an Internal Investigator, I developed an even greater sense of awareness and earned respect from leadership, believing this was my true calling. I worked closely with the Human Resources Department to ensure investigations were thorough, and I prided myself on being honest, developing genuine relationships with everyone. My husband—whom I met and dated in high school before we later married—has stood by my side through every chapter of life. He has always been my greatest supporter, encouraging me to pursue the career I believed in and never letting me lose sight of my path.

Of course, this job came with its challenges. I had my fair share of confrontations and altercations while protecting myself in a big city environment, and I was occasionally injured in the process, but it didn't stop me. At just 5'4", I often didn't look like someone who could be a threat, and I frequently found myself underestimated. As my husband and I discussed our future—starting a family and purchasing a home, which seemed impossible at the time—I then began to question whether law enforcement was truly my path.

One day, in the midst of a casual conversation with my Human Resources Manager at the time, I shared my uncertainties. She saw the strengths in me—my ability to connect with people, my strong work ethic—and as soon as she had an opening, she offered me the chance to transfer to her team. That moment marked the beginning of my journey into Human Resources, which is these days known as People Operations. I flourished in this new position, finding joy in learning, coaching others, advocating for fairness, and helping people navigate their careers. It was clear to me at last: I had found my true calling.

Not long after this career switch, we had our first child, and a few years later, began preparing for the arrival of our second. While we loved our city, San Francisco was prohibitively expensive even in the mid-2000s, even for people like us with great jobs. The houses we could afford to buy for our growing family were hours outside the city and needed lots of repairs. We knew if we were going to realize our dream of owning a home, we would have to move and settle somewhere else. So, we made the decision to start fresh in Arizona. We had family in Scottsdale and had always liked our visits to the desert. The housing market was beginning to take off in Arizona, and we saw it as an opportunity to get in quickly and give our children the kind of community and new home we had envisioned for them at a fraction of the cost of living in the Bay Area.

We took the leap, flew out to put down a deposit on a lot in a newly built family-focused community, and soon our home was being built. The process moved quickly. Before we knew it, I was saying goodbye to my hometown, my parents, sister, family, and close friends to embark on this new chapter. It was all about us, my husband and I, as a team focusing on our kids' future and the excitement of watching our new home take shape. While I missed the diversity of San Francisco, along with my close family and friends, we were confident Arizona was the right place for us at that stage in our lives. With the few amazing and supportive family members already settled in the Grand Canyon State, our adjustment was an amazing experience, and we are so thankful to them for their support.

As we settled into our new life, I gradually let go of the armor I had worn through my city years. It was wonderful to be in a place where I felt like I didn't need it anymore, yet years later, and still to this day, what bothers me the most is how unprepared I was on that specific June morning.

BLURRED BY FEAR

Looking back, the first night after that traumatic morning was a blur—sleepless, hollow, and filled with a sense of disconnection. The morning that followed felt like a nightmare I couldn't escape from. I felt detached from everything, as though I were a ghost walking through my own life. My gaze kept drifting to the window, where patrol cars sat parked outside, providing a small bit of comfort amidst the chaos. For the first time, all I wanted was to hold my children close and have my husband by my side, to feel the safety of his presence surrounding me.

The next day, reality came crashing back as I was taken by the detective on my case to meet with the sketch artist. The weight of my kidnapping grew heavier with each step, settling deeper in my chest. I remember the detective arriving to pick me up at my home, and together we drove to the sheriff's office, only a mile away. Once inside, we entered a small room where the sketch artist was waiting. The atmosphere was quiet and focused, as the artist began asking me about the details of the suspect's appearance. I struggled to remember every feature, the trauma clouding my mind. I could recall the general shape of his face, but it wasn't enough. I kept thinking back to that one moment I was able to glimpse his full face when his mask fell away for a split second. I had to close my eyes and concentrate hard, desperately trying to capture that fleeting image in my mind.

The artist started by asking about each facial feature—eyes, nose, mouth, and face shape—and I did my best to recall everything, but it became overwhelming. With each detail, I found myself second-guessing what I was describing. Did the eyes seem wide or narrow? Was the nose straight or slightly crooked? The more I tried to explain, the more the features blurred together, and I couldn't shake the feeling that I wasn't getting it right. Every time the artist made adjustments based on my feedback, I thought we were getting closer, but something still felt off. The face on the page didn't quite match the one I had seen in that brief, intense moment, but it was close. I could feel the weight of needing to get it right, yet despite all my efforts, the final image remained elusive—just a blur, like the edges of a dream.

The next day, my sketch was all over the local news, and the fear crept back in even stronger. Did

I get it right? And if so, what would it lead to? The reminder of the threats started to sink in again. My mind spiraled into an endless loop of "what ifs," each one more terrifying than the last. The fear, the uncertainty gnawed at me, draining the small bit of strength I had in me. On the outside, I tried to hold it together, to be strong like I always had in the face of adversity. But inside, the darkness was overwhelming.

The flood of calls, texts and social media messages became a constant reminder of what had happened and what was still unfolding. I had to recount the details to those closest to me, each conversation adding weight to my already fragile state. While I was grateful for the overwhelming support from friends and family, I struggled to fully absorb it. It felt too soon, too raw.

The community's outpouring of love was both comforting and suffocating. I've always been a chatty person—something my grammar school report cards never failed to note—so my friends were used to me talking a lot. But after everything I had just gone through, my mind was overloaded. I couldn't process it all at once. The emotional and mental strain made me realize the very support I had once embraced now felt more like a burden.

Don't get me wrong—I was incredibly grateful to those who checked in and offered their care and who were on a mission to help solve this case. I could see they genuinely wanted to help, to make sure I knew they were there if I needed to talk. But at that moment, I didn't know how to navigate the constant outpouring of concern. I struggled to express both my gratitude and my truth. When friends, my caring in-laws and my extended family asked how I was doing, or if I wanted to talk about it, I was at a loss. Every word I spoke felt heavy, as though I wasn't ready to share the full weight of what I was feeling. The only ones I felt like I could truly talk to were my husband and my mom and dad—but even then, I held back. They too were processing the gravity of what had happened, and I didn't want to add to their burden.

With my parents being a state away, I could feel their worry coming through the phone line. I remember being unable to communicate clearly, unable to find the words that would make sense of everything. I could sense their helplessness. There was nothing they could do, and for the first time, years later, I understood—really understood—what it must have been like for them. As a parent now, I could imagine the terror they must have felt, knowing their child was going through something so traumatic, and yet they couldn't just hop in the car and drive to provide comfort or protection. Even still, I probably wasn't ready for it yet, but I could feel their love and concern from miles away. I had always known they worried about me and my sister, even as adults, and I now saw it from a new perspective.

The constant, unshakeable worry that never goes away for parents—no matter how old their children get—became crystal clear. I realized no matter how old I was, or how independent I had become, they would always carry that concern for their daughters. And now, as a parent myself, I felt that same fear and helplessness in my own chest.

But as the days went on, I came to understand this support was not just a lifeline—it was essential.

My community—family, friends, coworkers, Russian River summer friends—continued to reach out, offering their support and even suggesting trips to help me escape my current surroundings. Part of me wanted to retreat as I first did, to continue handling this on my own, as I always had. But slowly, I began to let down my guard. My close friends, sensing my hesitation, continually respected my need for space but also encouraged me with quiet understanding.

Their patience, their willingness to let me move at my own pace, became a crucial part of my healing. Accepting their support was not easy, but it was necessary.

BUILDING MY CORE VALUES

Even as a young child, I have always been observant, analytical, and protective. I may not have been the most popular or the most academically gifted, but I had always surrounded myself with people who accepted me for who I was. The loyalty we shared, the bond we built, is something I still hold dear to this day. My friends, the ones who stood by me through thick and thin, were my strength; it wasn't just something I'd found in the aftermath of trauma— it had been there all along, cultivated by the love and support of those around me.

Growing up, I was fortunate to have two very close friends, Maria and Tara. Together, we formed an inseparable trio, "the three musketeers." We were always there to support one another. Despite our differences, we were typical kids, swiping each other's Barbie outfits, and we shared a deep sense of compassion, respect, and awareness for each other. Maria's father was also a firefighter, and her mother,

Rita, was that phenomenal mom everyone loved and who cared for all the neighborhood kiddos with a huge heart. Tara, who lived around the corner from me, also had a sister five years older than her. Our sisters were best friends, which connected us all a bit more. Tara was my unique and creative friend, and Maria was very by-the-book. While, like any group of ten-year-olds, we occasionally had moments of feeling left out, we always respected and cared for one another. The experiences we shared, both the good and the challenging, played a crucial role in shaping who I am today. I've come to realize these formative yet very different friendships not only helped me grow emotionally but also instilled in me the importance of supporting others in the same way.

The awareness I developed in those early years from my friendships with Maria and Tara and my summer family has grown with me and has crossed over into my career. The lessons I learned about collaboration, compassion, and support have been transformative, helping me navigate challenges and build meaningful connections with others. Having a strong support system makes all the difference in facing life's challenges. It's essential to remain open, connect with others, and step outside of your comfort zone. Sharing what I've learned and passing on those values to my team is incredibly rewarding, and it's a reminder of how powerful it can be to foster a supportive, connected environment, whether in childhood or in the workplace. Whether you're introverted or extroverted, a solid, supportive network is key to thriving.

WHERE THE HEALING BEGINS

These connections and care from others pushed me into a direction of immediate therapy.

As I think back to the options for therapy that were quickly made available to me after this incident, they became another key part of my journey. My employer at the time encouraged me to go, showing a level of care and concern I wasn't used to. They didn't just suggest I seek help—they took it a step further and paid for my sessions, covering the costs for both me and eventually for my daughter. It was humbling to see how much they cared—not just as my employer, but as people who were genuinely concerned for my well-being. Initially, I wasn't too keen on the idea of therapy. The fear of vulnerability and judgment didn't thrill me, and I didn't really understand how therapy could help someone.

Arriving at my first therapy session completely on my own, I had made the decision to drive there, despite feeling utterly drained, defeated, and scared. My guard was up, and I wasn't sure what to expect, or even how I would feel. Walking into the small office, I checked in at the station with the receptionist, and then sank into the visitor's couch still not believing I was sitting there at that moment. Amy, my therapist, with whom I immediately felt a calming and warm connection, began the process of guiding me through sharing my story. I tried to stay strong in front of this stranger, holding my vulnerability back, but as our conversation continued, I found it impossible to contain my emotions. Everything was so raw and fresh in my mind. It felt like I was watching video clips of haunting scenes that played over and over in my head. The experience was so current, so real, and I couldn't escape it.

We decided to add my daughter to the next session, and by then, I started to feel like the therapy was actually helping. I finally felt able to release the deep, painful details I had been guarding instead of suppressing my feelings. I was still very aware of the need to protect my loved ones from taking on any more burden. They needed to see me getting stronger, and in time, I slowly did. But I found solace in speaking to someone who could hold that weight for me, allowing me to take steps toward healing.

There was no judgment in therapy, only support, a new kind of community, and a new perspective on how to cope with the challenges life had thrown at me. I was so used to guarding and working through my own thoughts all this time that I'd missed out on the support of another perspective, other ideas that could've helped me.

A pivotal moment in my journey came when I realized how healing it was to talk through the events of my entire life and delve into the deep, sometimes uncomfortable, questions that helped me uncover the root causes of my struggles. This was a whole new level of vulnerability for me and part of why I hesitated to try therapy in the first place. But it was also a vulnerability that brought a sense of release—a way of unburdening the emotional weight I'd been carrying. As I became more open with those I trusted, I found myself shedding old scars and opening up in ways I hadn't before.

Long after I left therapy, I found a new way to grow by listening to podcasts. My daily commute to work pre-COVID was about a sixty-minute drive, and a friend had suggested I listen to the Lewis Howes podcast, *The School of Greatness*. That suggestion became a key part of my daily routine. Listening to the interviews felt like a private therapy session taking in what I could apply to my life at the time. Hearing about the struggles and triumphs of high-achieving guests kicked off my day with new thoughts and ideas. It all expanded my way of thinking and allowed my creativity to come out in my work and home life. It started to give me a new look and perspective on things and also sparked a bit of creativity that was sitting stagnant at the time. My fire was lit and started to burn, fueling me to grow faster as a person; something new was starting to take place.

As I continued my journey of healing, I found myself embracing my role as a leader and an advocate for others. In my career as an HR professional, I had always been the one to offer guidance, lift others up, and empower those around me, and this time of crisis reinforced the importance of that role even more. It gave me a renewed sense of purpose to be a louder voice for those who needed it, to stand up for the underdog, and to help others find their strength as my community had helped me find mine during difficult times. My job wasn't about the day to day work; it was about looking at someone and taking into account all they face and helping them holistically. And in doing so, I realized my journey was not only about my own growth but about helping those around me rise too—the desire to help those around me grow as well. It amplified my purpose.

FRACTURED BUT NOT BROKEN

Even as a kid, no matter what life threw my way, I always felt like I could take care of myself and protect others with my street smarts. I felt strong. I would sometimes encounter crazy situations or interesting individuals growing up in the city, but I felt confident handling them because I learned how to adapt and when to remove myself. I knew when to speak up and when to bite my tongue. I never felt unsafe. I was also always the first to lend a hand, offer genuine empathy, and show care for those around me. My ability to connect with others came from a place of heart—always seeking to understand, always ready to help. I built a network of solid friendships, and I developed a strong sense of character that allowed me to read people quickly. I trusted my instincts to steer me toward those who would become my true, supportive friends.

And in one single morning, all of that had been shattered—my sense of strength, my sense of safety, my role as protector, my place in my community— shattered, but not lost. It was still there. The trauma was a hard reminder of how interconnected we all are, and how the support of others can carry us through the darkest times. Doubling the pleasure of support and dividing the pain helped grow my resilience, my Titanium Strength, and propelled me forward, pushing me in a positive direction when it felt like everything else was falling apart. I wasn't alone, and that realization was everything.

Kidnapper sketch

Lori and Maria as kids

Tara and Lori as kids

House in Rio Nido, or what we called,
"The Russian River House"

CHAPTER 3

BUILDING RESILIENCE OVER TIME

After high school, I knew it was time to take charge of my health—physically and emotionally. The weight of relationships, work, starting college, and the overwhelming uncertainty of what the future held were beginning to feel like too much to carry.

Back when VHS tapes ruled the world, and Blockbuster was the go-to spot for Friday night rentals, I found myself unexpectedly wandering into the exercise section. It wasn't a place I'd ever really been before, but something about it caught my attention that day. That's when I spotted it: *The Original Buns of*

Steel. I vaguely remembered an infomercial I'd seen for it. I had no idea what to expect, but for some reason, it felt like the right choice—like fate. So, I grabbed the tape, paid for the rental, and headed home, eager to give it a try

I didn't have a proper fitness setup—just a thirteen-inch TV with a built-in VHS player perched on my dark wood dresser in the corner of my room and a small six-by-five space to work out on my bedroom carpet. I popped the tape in, hit play, and instantly embarked on what would turn out to be the first step in a life-altering journey—one that would take me from *Buns* to *Abs of Steel* and beyond. Health and fitness, things I'd never really paid so much attention to before, were about to become my new obsession. Exercise became my escape, and as I started to feel a shift in my confidence and energy, I committed to a routine.

I ended up purchasing my own new VHS copy; I was hooked. After a few weeks, I could complete those thirty-five minute workouts in my sleep. They weren't just about crunches and squats—they were my therapy, and something I looked forward to making the time each day to complete. Once I'd set a consistent routine, I chose to not shy away from it.

From there, I graduated to Tae Bo, feeling like I was ready to take on the world—or at least handle a few roundhouse kicks.

It was me in my room, stretching, kicking, and crunching in my little exercise space, no one judging my form. Just me and the instructor on the screen pushing through the workout together. I can still picture those moments even now.

When we moved to Arizona, I found a new sense of peace in the desert. The endless views and winding trails around our community became my sanctuary. I was still maintaining an exercise routine, and as an early riser, I started running every weekend. Gradually, I began pushing myself further and further, until I was covering distances I never thought possible. While my husband wasn't on the running bandwagon yet, I'd met a few local women through my son's soccer club who shared my passion and focus. We'd occasionally meet up and do short runs together.

It wasn't long before I made a bold decision: I was going to run a marathon. But not just any marathon—I was going to sign up for the Nike Marathon in San Francisco, a city that still felt like home. I remember the excitement that flooded through me when I was selected in the lottery, along with the thought of, *There's no turning back now.* A few of my local friends were selected too, as well as one of my high school friends, Melissa, with whom I had spent countless weekends.

Training for the marathon in Arizona's heat was grueling, especially during the summer months. On some mornings, I'd wake up at 3:30 a.m. to get going before the sun started to beat down. I'd drive to different corners of town to drop off water, so I'd have it when I passed by on my long runs. I'd be out there for hours, pushing through the heat and the miles, hearing my husband or my friends honk as they drove by to cheer me on. My mind was excited, but I was also filled with a deep, nervous determination. I couldn't afford to fail this mission—I was in it for the long haul.

When race day arrived, my husband was right there by my side, cheering me on, as he always is for me and my goals. Our friends came out to join us, some taking pictures at pivotal moments during our run, some showing up at various mile markers holding signs that read, "Just twenty-two more!" Their fun energy gave Melissa and me the strength we needed to keep going, and I felt their support with every step.

Between the steep inclines and my constant internal dialogue of *What was I thinking?*, it was getting tough. I had trained as best as I could in Arizona, finding the few hills and grades I could, but nothing prepared me for the beautiful and, at times, dreadful hills of San Francisco. But Melissa and I were alongside each other, pushing each other to stay focused and stick to our plan. We weren't stopping.

I had one goal in my head: I wasn't breaking. I wasn't stopping. I remember running at a snail's pace at times, but in my mind, I kept telling myself, *I'm not stopping!* I got in my own head and let the inner talk keep me going: *No way you're failing here, girl. You've got this!* Melissa's encouragement was the initial push I needed, and knowing she was by my side gave me the extra strength—especially as we hit mile twenty-two. When that surge of adrenaline finally kicked in, it felt like I had a clear, flat runway ahead of me, stretching down the Great Highway.

As we got closer to the finish line, we had gleaming smiles on our faces. No stops, no injuries—everything we had committed to separately in training was coming to fruition. We crossed that finish line with my husband and dear friends cheering us on. And in that moment, it hit me: the resilience I'd built, one *Buns of Steel* session at a time, was exactly what got me through those hills—and onto the next goal, and the next, along with the little pushes from my community.

Resilience, like muscle, doesn't grow overnight. It's built over time; through each challenge we face and each decision we make to keep moving forward. It's not an innate trait; it's a skill we develop as we navigate the ups and downs of life. Each struggle, whether personal or professional, is an opportunity to grow stronger, to deepen our capacity for endurance.

We don't always recognize it in the moment—sometimes, it takes years to realize how far we've come. It's those small moments of persistence, when we keep pushing forward despite the weight of the world or rise after what once felt like an insurmountable failure. It's like water slowly carving its path through stone; the pressure may not always be visible, but over time, it shapes us in ways we can't immediately see.

When we're younger, we face challenges that, in the grand scheme of things, might seem small—lost friendships, bad relationships, misunderstandings, the awkwardness of growing into ourselves. I was that kid with a lot of friends but still sometimes felt out of place, unsure of where I fit. My mind was constantly racing, and I had a hard time with test-taking and spelling, which made me an average student. I definitely wasn't the "standout"—except, of course, on the basketball court in grammar school, where I was small but mighty. My sense of self was like a puzzle I couldn't quite put together. But these moments, seemingly trivial at the time, are the first building blocks of resilience. We move through them without fully realizing how they're shaping us for the future. Yet, even in those quiet moments, the foundations of our strength are quietly being laid.

As life unfolds, those early struggles give way to more complex challenges: the sting of first heartbreaks, unraveling relationships, job losses, unexpected financial stress, or the devastating grief of losing someone close. We may find ourselves dealing with deeper emotional pain or enduring physical hardship. These are the moments that truly test our resilience and our Mental Fortitude. And yet, in the middle of it all, we often don't realize we're actually growing stronger. We don't always see how each hardship or even bit of success is preparing us for the larger battles that lie ahead. The strength we need to face tomorrow's obstacles is quietly being built today.

Eventually, this process creates something much more powerful than emotional toughness. It creates a kind of Titanium Strength—mental, emotional, and communal. Together, these elements form a holistic foundation for facing life's adversities. So often, we don't realize the hardships of today are the very experiences that will equip us to handle the trials of tomorrow. But as we keep moving, we build the Titanium Strength we'll need to not just survive but thrive.

DISCOVERING UNKNOWN STRENGTH

Before I understood the power of Titanium Strength or before I even recognized it as a strength, the voice that kept me going through the challenges of life and the kidnapping was just that—the nameless voice of my guardian angel or my intuition or whatever it is. As the month passed after my kidnapping, when I was still trying to find my footing, I had a moment that shifted something deep within me. It was early morning, just me and the road. I was on my way to work, the streets quiet and empty, the day still new.

I wasn't thinking much—just trying to get through the motions and awareness on the road. The radio played softly in the background, the familiar hum of traffic the only company I had. That's when "Titanium" by David Guetta and Sia came on.

At first, I barely noticed, just letting the beat fill the space, but then the lyrics hit: "I'm bulletproof, nothing to lose." As I mentioned in Chapter 1, it was like a lightbulb suddenly turned on. The words spoke straight to my heart. I sat up a little straighter in my seat, my hands gripping the wheel. It was like the song had come on at exactly the right time, like it was meant for me. *Titanium.* The word itself was heavy, like a weight I could finally carry. I thought about everything I'd been through, the things that had broken me, and realized I wasn't shattered. I had survived. I was still standing.

It wasn't only the music or the beat—it was the message. It washed over me, a wave of strength I didn't know I had. It was as if that song had been waiting for me to remind me that I could keep going, I could rebuild. And from that moment on, whenever I faced tough days or needed a little push, "Titanium" showed up again and again, as if the universe knew exactly when I needed to hear it most. It became my anthem, a reminder that I was unbreakable. Its powerful words gave me the strength to face each day, helping me rebuild my confidence and reclaim my independence.

Every lyric resonated with me, echoing my emotions from the recent trauma, while also reaching deeper into my past. It reminded me of the challenges I had overcome before and the resilience I had cultivated over the years. The song became more than just a reminder of what I was enduring in the present—it was a call to remember the strength within me that had always been there, guiding me through life's toughest battles.

As time passed, "Titanium" gradually transformed into a family mantra—a reference only we shared, a private symbol of strength we turned to during difficult times. When life threw what seemed like its hardest challenges our way, we would lean into those lyrics, finding courage in the reminder that we were resilient, unbreakable, and stronger than we ever imagined. It became our quiet, unspoken rally cry. We didn't share it with anyone else, but it was a bond that held us together, reminding us, no matter what, we could face any challenge with unyielding strength.

Watching my children face challenges with the same inner strength I had cultivated throughout my life was a reminder that my journey had not just been for me. It was for them, too, and was something I had learned from my fierce mother and father.

I saw this strength reflected in my daughter as she navigated her way through the ups and downs of high school and college. When drama, setbacks, or moments of feeling left out threatened her peace, I found her turning to the words of "Titanium," using it to take the high road and rise above the noise. That's when I realized something powerful: The resilience that had helped me through my own struggles had been passed down to her. The strength I had fought for and built over the years was being reflected in her. The environment she grew up in, different from my own childhood, had shaped her, but it also gave her the tools to face adversity with grace and determination.

It was in my son's journey as well—his high school years, impacted by the isolation of the COVID pandemic. A young man who had once been the little guy with the highest spirit and the kindest heart, my son's high school experience was stripped of the social interactions that typically shape those years. He grew up as a club soccer player, each year meeting many new teammates from different schools, so he never truly found the close-knit friendships my husband and I had enjoyed as children. And being the "little guy" for many years in a competitive sport had its ups and downs. We had our experience of being around some amazing families and kids during this period that we still connect with today, but the connections for my son's friendships weren't there the way we would have loved to see them during grammar and high school years.

The days of riding bikes through the neighborhood, gathering with friends on a whim, were the norm in my childhood but much different from his. In the absence of this social connection, I watched my son grapple with the isolation at times, struggling with the deep yearning for the friendships and experiences during those critical years, and turning to a digital world. He went from the little guy with amazing foot skills on the soccer field, which gets a bit more challenging in the later years of high school, to a last-minute growth spurt, and suddenly, he was six feet tall after high school but now burned out from the field.

As a parent, I had always been open, yet cautious, balancing my own experiences with the awareness of how different the world was for my children. My own childhood, filled with endless opportunities for spontaneous socializing, was now a far cry from what my son knew—his formative years spent navigating a virtual world, unable to truly bond in the way I had. But "Titanium" became his silent reminder, too; despite the challenges, he was unbreakable, capable of navigating the tough years of isolation and would ultimately emerge stronger than before.

The song "Titanium," which had been my personal anthem, became a shared reminder of how mental, emotional, and communal strength, resilience, and perseverance could carry us through anything. It was a lesson we passed on, not only to each other but to the next generation as well.

THE PILLARS OF TITANIUM STRENGTH

Many years have now passed since the kidnapping. Looking back on this journey, I've pinpointed three key factors that have shaped this Titanium Strength: Mental Fortitude, Emotional Flexibility, and Community Support.

Mental Fortitude: Finding that ability to stay focused, determined, and positive, even when life throws its toughest challenges at you. It's about pushing through difficult times, maintaining discipline, and persevering without giving up. Mental Fortitude can show up in many ways—whether you're training for a marathon or simply working toward a personal goal, like running that first mile. Everyone's journey is different.

For me, an example of Mental Fortitude meant dealing with test anxiety for years, something that resurfaced as an adult. Life is full of setbacks like financial struggles, job losses, or unexpected challenges, and it's through these moments we truly learn to build strength and resilience. Facing these difficulties head-on and finding ways to manage them is part of how I've learned to cultivate my Mental Fortitude.

Emotional Flexibility: Adapting and managing your emotions as life changes around you. It's about staying resilient—letting yourself feel your emotions without letting them take over, and learning to move forward in a balanced way.

Life is constantly changing—relationships shift, work environments change—we face disappointments or experience losses that test us in ways we never imagined. Whether it's the loss of a loved one, dealing with failure, or adjusting to life's difficult changes, learning how to navigate these shifts is never easy. But it's through Emotional Flexibility that we learn to not just survive but thrive through these challenges.

Community Support: Opening up and letting others in. It's a powerful factor in building that Titanium Strength. One of my favorite steps in my own journey has been learning the importance of leaning on others. We all need support, but sometimes we have to make a conscious effort to tap into the Community around us, recognize the help that's available, and take the leap to expand our network.

The connections we make with others are essential—they empower us, help us stay grounded, and build resilience, especially during tough times.

Once I identified these factors, I began to see how each experience in my life—whether it was my childhood struggles, my constant focus on observing, or the empowering moments from those around me—has helped shape the Titanium Strength I carry with me today. Being observant and aware of my surroundings has played a major role in my personal growth, as it allows me to learn and adapt along the way. Surrounding myself with a supportive Community has been a key factor in my healing, boosting my confidence, and helping me feel empowered to handle anything that comes my way.

Over the next few chapters, I'll continue to take you through my journey of Titanium Strength, showing you the power of Mental Fortitude, Emotional Flexibility, and Community Support. We all have this strength, even if we don't realize it. And when we tap into it, we become bulletproof.

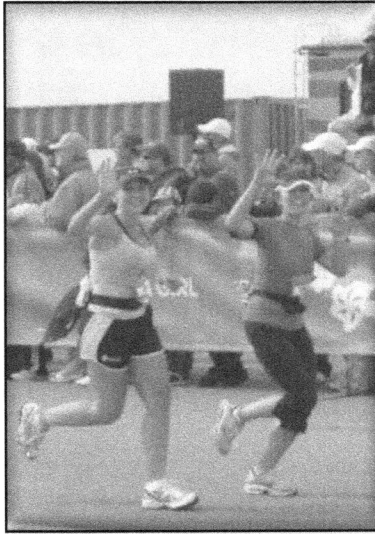

Nike Marathon Photos with Melissa

CHAPTER 4

MENTAL FORTITUDE IN REAL LIFE

In 2011, with the kidnapping still at the forefront of my mind, the usual excitement of summer vacation day camps and activities ended for the kids. As the school year kicked off, I began to feel like things were slowly starting to turn a corner for me. I was growing more comfortable with the success of the small milestones I had been achieving on my own. Some days, I even mustered up the strength to lay out my gym clothes before going to bed so I wouldn't have an excuse to miss a morning workout at the local community center where I could zone in on my exercises with friends. Exercise has always been great for my mental health, and I wanted to get back to it.

Our family returned quickly to the daily routine of waking up extremely early to get the kids ready for before-school care, then dropping them off for their early morning program before my husband and I headed to our jobs. Frankly, we were busy, and there was no choice for me to sit and fall into a deep hole. I had to push forward. I went on as best as I could and checked them in at 6:15 a.m. every morning with their favorite before-school teacher, Mrs. Theresa. I'd give them a kiss goodbye and then jump back in the car for my typical thirty-minute drive to the office. The route was quiet down a long, four-lane road with the music low and the morning calm.

Then it happened.

A motorcyclist sped up behind me, wearing a dark bandana around his nose and mouth and coincidentally with a similar stature to the man I had previously encountered. Moments later, a white Nissan Altima—exactly the same make and model of the car that had followed me *that* morning—whizzed by. Not only was it the same make and color, but the tinted windows were nearly identical, making it even more unsettling.

I went numb.

Instantly, I slowed down and grasped my cell phone, holding it ready. *What were the chances?* The timing was uncanny. At that moment, I mentally hit a bump in the road.

Was this a test? I fought back the tears filling my eyes. It wasn't easy, especially when I thought things were finally starting to improve, and then this trigger hit me.

Since the kidnapping, each time I had seen a bandana, my heart would race, and a tightness would grip my chest out of nowhere. But I learned to breathe deeply, to talk to myself in the quietest way, to control the surge of emotion. I wouldn't let it take over, but it was a constant battle. The timing of this incident just hit harder than what I had been experiencing for some reason.

I continued to head to work and parked in my usual spot close to the office door. I turned off the engine and took a moment to breathe, still holding back tears. *I am safe. I am safe.* Once the beating of my heart slowed down, I walked into the building to start my day. However, I kept the stress of that drive to myself, going on with my work day, not wanting to alarm my family, who were still navigating their own healing.

When I ran the marathon in San Francisco all those years ago, crossing that finish line wasn't just about physical endurance. Sure, the training had its fair share of grueling miles and extremely early and hot mornings in the desert training for the big day, but what got me through those steep hills and relentless fatigue wasn't just my legs. It was the mental strength I had been building subconsciously, one *Buns of Steel* session at a time, and more intentionally, one mile at a time, as I prepared for the marathon.

Pushing my body to the limit forced me to confront my mind. At some point, the physical discomfort faded into the background, and all that was left was the mental game. I wasn't running those hills with my legs alone; I was battling against the doubts in my mind, the fear of failure, and the voice that said, "What the hell were you thinking?"

This is where Mental Fortitude came into play.

Whether it was the early mornings of training, the endless repetitions of exercises that seemed pointless at the time, or the quiet moments in the race where I wondered if I could go on—every moment tested my ability to stay calm, focused, and determined. It wasn't just about the destination; it was about having the mental strength to keep going when my body said no, to push through when I couldn't see the finish line, and to stay true to my goal, even when the path was unclear.

And that's when I realized: Mental Fortitude isn't something you're born with; it's built over time. It's forged in the quiet moments when you make the choice to keep going. It's built in the moments when no one is watching, and it becomes the secret weapon that helps you achieve the impossible.

As I sat at my desk that morning after seeing the motorcyclist wearing the bandana, I realized I was tapping into this Mental Fortitude. And I knew I could get through, as I always had before, because I'd unknowingly spent years preparing for this moment.

THOSE WHO INSPIRE US ALONG THE WAY

Resilience born from Mental Fortitude is something we witness every day—in the lives of our friends, families, and public figures. As a child, I was often surrounded by strong, unwavering figures, particularly in the lives of my family. I watched as these figures faced the highs and lows of life, learning what it meant to persevere and remain steadfast, even in the face of hardship. Much of my childhood was marked by the presence of older relatives, many of whom I would lose over time, attending countless funerals that left a lasting impression on me.

I was about ten years old when my mother, sensing something was wrong, told me we needed to go check on my Grandpa Joe. He hadn't answered her calls, and she was becoming increasingly worried. My grandfather was a sweet Irishman born in Sligo in 1910 who migrated to the US and made an impact on San Francisco. He was the main grandparent in my life at that young age. As a grandpa, he was the one I felt connected to and who had always been there for me after school. He lived just three doors down from my best friend Maria, and I adored him. His daily routine and quiet and comforting presence made him a rock on my mom's side of our family.

When my mother and I arrived at his house, I walked in first. That's when I found him, lying alongside his bed, his church clothes still neatly pressed, his bathroom sink still filled with water from his morning shave, his routine frozen in time. He had passed away.

But it wasn't just the fact of the loss of my grandfather that hit me; it was the profound sadness that weighed on me. Even still, I found myself more focused on my mother. I could see a silence heavier than words settled around us. I saw the shock wash over her—grief, disbelief, and a kind of heartbreak you can never be prepared for, the kind that only comes from losing the person who once held your hand through life—yet as I watched, she sprang into action, navigating the next steps with a strength I had never before witnessed.

I think it was at that very moment that my own strength was forged. My mother, in the face of such deep personal loss, didn't crumble. She acted swiftly, determinedly, showing a resilience that, in hindsight, was nothing short of heroic. I witnessed firsthand what it meant to face the unexpected with unwavering resolve.

I grabbed the rotary phone with the never ending cord to call 911, my mental state calm but my hands shaking, as my mom rushed next door to Maria's house to see if her dad could help—leaving me there with my grandfather. I froze standing alongside him. Everything was happening so quickly, so unexpectedly, but somehow, despite my age, I too found a way to swing into action, to adapt. Looking back, I know the events that unfolded that day shaped my ability to handle life's challenges with grace and resilience.

The loss of my Grandpa Joe was devastating, a blow to our family we would carry with us for years to come. He left a lasting impression on all he came in contact with. Yet, even in the midst of that grief, I saw strength—not just in my mother but in myself as well—a strength forged from the example of those around me. It's this kind of inner fortitude I carry with me today, a reminder that sometimes, strength is born from the most difficult of moments.

Along with my mom, I'm fortunate to be surrounded by incredible individuals who've displayed remarkable resilience, overcoming challenges such as health issues, divorce, addiction, loss, and childhood trauma. When I find myself struggling or feeling stuck, unable to see past the challenge at hand, I look to these people for inspiration. One person who always comes to mind is my best friend, Maria. She faced an unimaginable loss when her mother, Rita, who I've mentioned before as the "Mom-to-Everyone," passed away suddenly as Maria was about to start eighth grade. Losing a mother at such a crucial age is devastating. The absence of someone who was not just a mother but a constant source of love, guidance, and support creates a void that feels impossible to fill.

During those pivotal high school years, when a young girl needs her mother more than ever—to share victories, navigate challenges, or simply have someone to lean on—Maria had to face the heart-wrenching reality of losing that presence. Despite the immense grief, she exhibited quiet strength. As her mind tried to process such an abrupt loss, Maria had to find a way to continue moving forward, navigating life without the woman who had been her anchor. While her community, friends, and family stepped in to support, this twelve year-old girl was suppressing her feelings and grappling with the loss on her own, relying on her inner strength to carry her through. It wasn't until years later after an emotional breakthrough with her father that the depth of her pain was fully revealed. They had both been battling their emotions on their own, and opening up to each other strengthened their bond.

I deeply admire Maria for how she handled the loss. She could have easily chosen a different path, but instead, her resilience pushed her to keep moving forward. In times of tragedy, relationships often shift, and in this case, it eventually made Maria's relationship with her dad even stronger. Her ability to continue, despite the absence of her mother, is a testament to the depth of her resilience in the face of unimaginable loss.

Years later, Maria became a mother herself, blessed with twin daughters. In raising them, she has embodied the strength, love, and support her own mother gave her. She nurtures her girls with the same care and dedication, passing on the love and wisdom she received from her mother, now doubled. Through her journey, Maria has become the mother she once needed, channeling that strength to provide the foundation she herself was given—even in the moments when she needs her own mother's perspective the most, despite the fact she's no longer there.

Another lesson in Mental Fortitude was my father's battle with ALS, which began after we'd settled into life in Arizona. Dad had retired after dedicating thirty-five years to the City of San Francisco—starting as a Cement Mason before transitioning to the San Francisco Fire Department, where he spent twenty-eight years serving his city. After retirement, he and Mom moved across the Bay to a quieter, more peaceful home. With my sister, aunt, and uncle nearby, their days were filled with frequent visits, weekly dinners, and the warmth of family. Even in retirement, Dad remained his handy, resourceful self—always fixing things, maintaining the house, and, of course, cooking amazing meals, though now for a smaller crowd than the firehouse.

But as the years passed, Dad's health began to decline. Simple errands became slower, and though he remained determined to stay active, it was clear something was changing. He still made time for everything, especially bonding with my nephew Kevin, always determined to be the strong grandpa we knew him to be. Even when frustration surfaced, his heart remained the same.

Then, more troubling signs appeared. The man who had once been a force of nature—strong, confident, and full of life—began to fade. His energy diminished, and everyday tasks became more difficult. The changes were slow at first, subtle enough to dismiss as part of aging, but COVID made getting medical help nearly impossible. His symptoms were vague and inconsistent, making them hard to pinpoint. His most noticeable complaint was his neck tilting forward, gradually worsening over time. He needed more assistance getting in and out of the car, moved more slowly, and his appetite declined.

We did everything we could to adapt. My sister, always proactive, started researching and finding tools to make his life easier—mobility aids, adaptive equipment, even neck braces for different times of the day. She adjusted his meals to boost his caloric intake, determined to slow the weight loss. At the time, we were just problem-solving on our own, unaware of what was truly happening. By the time he finally saw a neurologist, the reality was devastating.

After countless doctor visits and even firefighters coming to help him up after falls, Dad was diagnosed with Amyotrophic Lateral Sclerosis (ALS). Also known as Lou Gehrig's disease, ALS is a progressive neurodegenerative condition that attacks nerve cells in the brain and spinal cord. It weakens muscles, steals mobility, and eventually affects speaking, swallowing, and breathing.

The diagnosis was a shock. ALS is difficult to diagnose even under normal circumstances, and COVID only prolonged the process. The disease moves swiftly, leaving little time between diagnosis and its final stages. By then, the simple act of lifting his head was no longer possible. Every day was another battle as his body continued to betray him. Despite this, he fought—holding onto his spirit, cherishing every moment he had with us.

Dad, once a man of many words, became quieter. He seemed bewildered by the changes in his body, struggling to comprehend what was happening to him. Being a state away, I felt helpless, much like my parents must have felt when they were far from me during difficult times. Who was there to step in? My sister.

She was the unsung hero, her strength hidden behind her own struggles. Even before the diagnosis, she spent hours researching ways to keep Dad comfortable, constantly searching for new tools, routines, and medical solutions. Every visit home, I'd see the garage filled with yet another contraption meant to help him navigate his new reality. She was tireless, ensuring he had everything he needed.

What makes her strength even more incredible is that she was fighting her own battle—recovering from cancer, a fight she kept mostly to herself. Instead of focusing on her own pain, she turned her attention to Dad. Looking back, I realize now how similar we are—how we both developed a quiet resilience that helped us push through difficult moments.

If you want to talk about a superhero, it was her. She showed up for everyone, even when she was struggling. She carried the weight of it all, making sure everything was taken care of while Mom was still reeling from the shock of how quickly life had changed.

For Mom, the hardest part was watching the love of her life—the strong, capable man she had always leaned on—transform into someone fragile and unrecognizable. The foundation of their life together, built on his unwavering strength, was crumbling. The pain of watching him fade was unbearable, and there was nothing any of us could do to stop it.

In July 2021, my father lost his battle with ALS. My mom, my sister, and I were by his side, saying goodbye. It was one of the hardest moments of our lives. But as painful as it was, I know he found peace. Even now, in life's hardest moments, I still feel his presence.

Writing this exact chapter today, on my Dad's birthday, feels like more than a coincidence. It's a reminder he's still here, cheering me on, offering his silent support. His journey, though heartbreaking, taught us all about resilience—not the kind that pretends everything is fine, but the kind that faces pain head-on and pushes forward anyway. Through it all, we learned strength isn't about carrying burdens alone. It's about the people who show up—the friends, family, doctors, caregivers, and even strangers who stepped in when we needed them most. Their love reminded us that even in loss, we are never truly alone.

As we move forward, we carry with us the lessons Dad taught us about love and perseverance. And I honor him by living with the same resilience he showed every day. Because in the end, it's not just about surviving the hard times—it's about the people who stand beside us, keeping love and memories alive.

While inspiration often flows from family, sometimes the most powerful spark comes from a complete stranger. Our loved ones may shape who we are, but it's often the people we least expect who help us unlock our potential.

One such person for me is Ed Mylett—a renowned entrepreneur, motivational speaker, and podcast host. I initially stumbled upon his work by chance, but what I found was transformative. Known for his expertise in peak performance and personal development, Ed uses his platform, *The Ed Mylett Show*, to interview high achievers and inspire others to live with intention and purpose.

What makes Ed truly inspiring is his openness about the battles he's faced. From growing up in a rough neighborhood to wrestling with self-doubt and inadequacy, he turned his challenges into fuel for growth. His journey isn't just about success—it's about giving back, lifting others up, and showing that even the toughest beginnings don't define our endings. I later had the honor of meeting Ed, and that experience only deepened my respect for the authenticity and strength he radiates.

But the only reason I found Ed Mylett's work in the first place was through someone else—Lewis Howes, whose mission is to inspire greatness in others. Back in Chapter 2, I mentioned finding Lewis's podcast, *The School of Greatness*. Since becoming an avid listener, I've had the honor of meeting Lewis multiple times, and every encounter leaves me more inspired. His books—*The School of Greatness*, *The Mask of Masculinity*, and most recently, *Make Money Easy*—explore the core of self-improvement: healing, vulnerability, emotional strength, and financial transformation. Lewis's story of facing and healing from childhood trauma is courageous and has made a deep impact on me. Through therapy, reflection, and honesty, he's modeled what it looks like to turn pain into purpose.

His work has introduced me to a Community of like-minded individuals striving to grow, heal, and lead with heart. This Community—alongside Lewis's consistent message of resilience—has shifted my life's course. I look forward to diving deeper into how this transformation has unfolded in future chapters.

Alongside Ed and Lewis, another figure whose story resonated deeply with me is Daymond John, the founder of FUBU, and now one of the Sharks on *Shark Tank*. Like me, he was raised by a strong family who prioritized education. Both of our families made sacrifices to send us to Catholic school, planting early seeds of discipline, faith, and perseverance.

One of the things that stood out most to me in Daymond's story was the strength of his mother— her unwavering belief in him, her tough love, and her refusal to let him settle for less. That fierce maternal strength reminded me so much of my own mother, who, through her actions more than her words, instilled in me a deep work ethic, a strong sense of responsibility, and constant encouragement. Daymond's journey—from hustling homemade hats from his mother's house to building a global brand—

is undeniably inspiring. But it's the foundational values he was raised with—the same ones I know so well—that truly hit home. This grassroots, home-based hustle is a core part of the FUBU origin story and a powerful example of resourcefulness, family support, and the belief of a community.

Behind the bold letters of FUBU is a man with Titanium Strength, someone who carries vision and resilience through every stage of the journey. He has faced countless rejections but turned each one into a stepping stone. And he hasn't done it alone.

He built FUBU alongside a close-knit community—friends who believed in the dream and local supporters who took a chance on his vision. That collective belief helped bring the brand to life. Years later, Daymond has used his platform on *Shark Tank* to do the same for others—investing in everyday dreamers and helping them rise. That full-circle moment—from a young man lifted by his community to a mentor changing lives—is what true impact looks like.

Through individuals like Ed, Lewis, and Daymond and the stories they've courageously shared, I've been reminded that greatness often begins in struggle. Their voices, platforms, and paths introduced me to a powerful community of people committed to growth, healing, and heart-led leadership who I continue to learn from and be inspired by everyday.

ADJUSTING IN THE WORKPLACE

Throughout my twenty-five-year career as a Human Resources professional across diverse industries, one of the most valuable skills I've honed is the ability to adapt to change—quickly, intentionally, and with resilience. In today's fast-paced, ever-evolving workplace, this isn't just a bonus—it's essential. The days of predictable, routine job descriptions are long gone. In their place are roles that demand agility, emotional intelligence, and a steady mindset. Change happens fast, and in those moments, Mental Fortitude isn't optional—it's everything.

As a leader, one of my greatest passions is helping others build that same resilience. I advocate fiercely for those I lead, guiding them through moments of uncertainty with genuine care and consistent encouragement so they can thrive not only as professionals but as whole people. Human Resources often gets a bad rap, seen as bureaucratic or impersonal, but in truth, it holds immense potential to nurture strength, trust, and authentic human connection. When HR is grounded in empathy and support, it evolves from a corporate function to a lifeline—an ally in personal and organizational growth.

I've been fortunate throughout my journey to have mentors and leaders who truly saw me, who challenged me to grow and who believed in me even before I fully believed in myself. Their belief often came in the form of a gentle nudge to lead with the creative ideas I began to share, to hype me up, and to remind me *I've got this*. Sometimes, it was the push I needed to step out from the crowd of executive leaders and put myself out there. That kind of support didn't just build my confidence—it fortified my mindset. It gave me the mental resilience to take risks, face challenges, and trust my voice. That kind of belief is powerful. It stays with you—and I've carried it with me, doing my best to pay it forward.

These moments have left a lasting imprint. They remind me that showing up—fully, compassionately, and without hesitation—is an act of Mental Fortitude. And that kind of presence? It can change everything.

THE STRENGTH OF FACING OUR PAIN

Life has a way of knocking us off balance. We all have moments when we're just trying to hold it together, unsure if we can make it through the day. But this is where Mental Fortitude steps in. It's the quiet strength that whispers, "You can do this," even when you're overwhelmed. It doesn't mean pretending you're okay—it means choosing to face what hurts and still taking that next step. It's the steady climb from surviving to thriving.

I've learned that if we avoid our pain, we only delay our healing. But if we face it—triggers, grief, trauma and all—we begin to reclaim our power. I remember how something as simple as a bandana or seeing a Nissan Altima could send me spiraling. But over time, I began to take my strength back—one trigger at a time. I refused to let those moments define me. It was a slow, intentional battle—but one I was determined to win.

Mental Fortitude isn't something you're born with—it's forged through fire. You build it in moments of challenge, uncertainty, and quiet courage. And once you've built it, it becomes your anchor—your shield—your inner compass for navigating anything life throws your way.

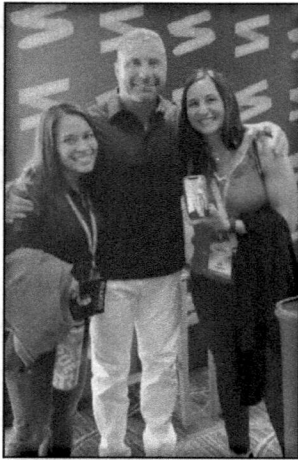

Picture with Ed Mylett, Michelle,
Lori, and Michelle on Facetime

Lori and Dad

Mom, Lori, Sister Lisa, and Dad

Dad with the grandkids (left to
right: Josh, Gianna, and Kevin)

Lori and Dad

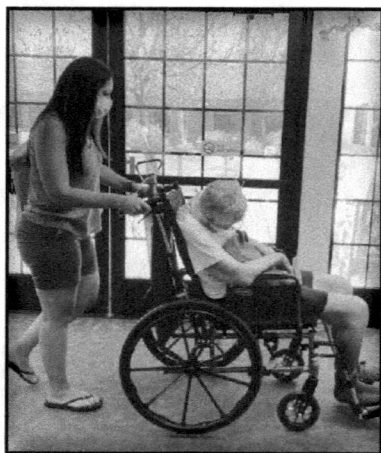

Lori and Dad

CHAPTER 5

EMOTIONAL FLEXIBILITY AND THE POWER TO HEAL

When the world shut down in 2020, I found myself holding two vastly different emotional truths at the same time. One of my children was suddenly schooling from home, their routine and social world upended overnight, while the other, just stepping into the long-awaited dream job and what she saw as a solid step forward in her future, had it pulled from underneath her. My husband and I had to be the steady ground beneath both of them, even as I felt the earth shift beneath my own feet. I allowed space for their disappointment, confusion, and grief, while managing my own behind closed doors. Emotional Flexibility, I learned, wasn't about staying strong all the time—it was about being soft enough to bend, to shift, to adapt without breaking.

Every morning, I put on a brave face for the video calls, the team meetings, and the kids' virtual classes. I spoke with calm, gave direction, and offered encouragement. I showed up as the dependable leader at work and the steady parent at home. But behind that composed exterior, my heart ached watching my kids wrestle with the weight of uncertainty. My youngest tried to stay engaged with school through a screen, his energy dimming a little more each day. My eldest, full of hope just weeks before, was left disoriented and deflated by the loss of her dream job and experience. I wanted to fix it for them, to make it all right, but I couldn't. And so, I did the only thing I could: I held the space. I was the strong one on the outside, and quietly, the soft one within.

The way I was raised—always active, always adapting—instilled in me a mindset of perseverance. I set small goals, celebrated milestones, and remained determined not to let anyone down. I knew I had to adapt, and somehow, I did. I focused on being the support for our kids, as my parents had been the support for me.

Instead of seeking control over the uncontrollable, I focused on being present. I adjusted my expectations of what success looked like each day. I became a part-time teacher, a late-night listener, a full-time emotional anchor. Behind the strong exterior, I allowed myself to cry when I needed to, laugh when I could, and sit quietly when words felt inadequate. Through it all, I didn't chase certainty—I chased connection. In doing so, I discovered a strength far more enduring than grit: the courage to move with change, not against it.

THE HEART OF BEING

My husband and I were young when we married in 1997. At the age of twenty-two, we had a whole lot of life in front of us. The early years were filled with learning the rhythms of marriage—growing together through our struggles, our triumphs, and the simple act of becoming a team. Through it all, one thing remained clear: We were ready to start a family. Our dreams of parenthood, however, were tempered with patience and hope.

In 1999, we had our first child, and our world changed forever. The joy of becoming parents was indescribable—the kind of joy that fills your home with laughter and makes even the most mundane moments feel miraculous. Her first steps. Her first words. The way she looked up at us with wide, curious, big brown eyes full of wonder. We had done it. We were parents. It was the dream we had always imagined but never fully believed would come true until it did.

On that Thanksgiving Day when Gianna made her grand entrance into the world, our families gathered to celebrate the holiday, eagerly awaiting the news. My dad, never one to miss out on a family tradition, smuggled a full Thanksgiving dinner into the hospital, delicately packing each dish into separate containers. I couldn't help but laugh as I sat there, bearing through the pain and nibbling on my ice chips. That was my dad—always bringing joy, always giving. I was about to give birth, but he made sure my husband was fed a great meal to celebrate this glorious celebration.

The moment Gianna was born, she immediately captured the hearts of everyone. She was our energetic, outgoing angel. She was the first grandchild on both sides of the family, and the love poured in like a flood. Our parents, reliving the joy of parenthood, spoiled her with affection and care. As we navigated those early moments of parenthood, our families were there, guiding us, offering support, and celebrating with us. It felt like the beginning of something beautiful.

After these first few years of Gianna's life, we quickly found ourselves ready to expand our family. Soon after making this decision, we found out we were expecting again. We had a quiet confidence. We'd done it once. We knew what to expect. We were ready. But life, in its unpredictable way, had other plans.

The scheduled ultrasound after the multiple pregnancy tests was supposed to be a confirmation of our second child—a sibling for Gianna, a new life we had already begun to dream about. But the moment the doctor's face shifted, I knew. The words, "I'm so sorry," fell heavy and final. Just like that, our dreams crumbled.

The joy we'd felt so certain of slipped away, leaving in its place an aching silence. I looked at my husband, and though our faces were filled with the same sorrow, there were no words. It was the first time we'd shared this kind of loss together. In that moment, we both felt adrift, caught in a sea of grief and confusion.

We'd had our first child. We had made it through the sleepless nights and the overwhelming joy. And now, we had lost the second; the one we never thought we could lose.

When a mother experiences a miscarriage, the grief is often overwhelming. The loss feels profound, creating both a physical and emotional emptiness. The question lingers: Could I have done something differently? It's impossible to answer, especially when you know deep down there was nothing more you could have done.

For my husband, watching me experience this heartbreak created a different kind of grief. He felt a deep, helpless sorrow. The future he had imagined for us—teaching our children, watching them grow, sharing those milestones—was suddenly lost. He, too, had to mourn, but he did so in a way that was quiet, often hidden beneath the surface, as he shouldered the role of being strong for me.

We both went through the sadness, but we had Gianna—our beautiful, healthy girl—who gave us something to hold on to. I leaned into the beauty we had with Gianna and thought of other beautiful moms who might not have had the simple experience of pregnancy even once. We decided to try again, and soon, we found out we were expecting once more.

This time, we saw the ultrasound, heard the heartbeat, and everything seemed perfect. The baby was growing inside me, healthy and strong. I was in the best shape, both physically and emotionally, ready for the next chapter. And yet, it stopped—the baby's development halted. I found myself facing another miscarriage, once again, with my husband by my side.

This second loss was harder to bear. Each time, the grief grew deeper. I remember trying to hold back the tears, to appear strong, though inside I was breaking. I had always been the one to solve problems, to support others through their challenges, but I couldn't this time. Even in my grief, I knew I had to let my husband grieve in his own way.

One summer evening, as we wrapped up dinner at our family cabin at the Russian River, my husband was outside with Gianna. Inside, my mother, who always seemed to know when something was stirring beneath the surface, pulled me aside. She was joined by my aunt Carol—full of energy, warmth, and always a source of joy. She co-owned the cabin with my mom, and over the years, she had become a second mother to me. These two strong, beautiful women had always been my anchors—steadfast and close, showing up time and time again when I needed them most.

That evening, with grief settling over me like a heavy blanket, I finally let the words spill out. I spoke of the sadness I'd been carrying—the pain of not being able to have another child, the quiet but persistent disappointment that clung to me, and how I had begun to carry the weight of others' unspoken emotions, especially my husband's. I've always been someone who anticipates problems, who steps in early to make things right. But this was a challenge I couldn't outmaneuver or fix.

As I opened up, my mother and aunt didn't interrupt or try to smooth anything over. They just listened—fully, patiently, without judgment. It was my mom who gently broke the silence, opening up about her own past. She shared losses I had never known about—losses that had shaped her in quiet, enduring ways. There was no bitterness in her voice, only a grace that came from living through sorrow and somehow finding a way to move forward with softness still intact.

My aunt didn't offer a story of her own, but her encouragement was no less powerful. Her words were steady and uplifting, like a gentle hand on my back. She reminded me I wasn't alone, I was strong even when I didn't feel it, and healing doesn't come on a schedule. She reminded me that leaning on those who love you isn't weakness—it's human.

Together, they created a space that felt safe. I didn't feel the pressure to be okay—I was simply allowed to be. Their support didn't make the grief disappear, but it helped me carry it. For the first time in a long while, the weight didn't feel like mine alone.

That weekend at the cabin was quiet, almost still. And in that stillness, surrounded by their care, my mind turned inward. I began to wonder if maybe there was a bigger picture. Perhaps things really do unfold for a reason—a belief I had never fully embraced until then. It's not always a comforting thought. In fact, it can feel cruel in the moment. But slowly, I started to see that sometimes, no matter how deeply we want something, it simply isn't meant for now. And somehow, in that space of letting go, a fragile but honest sense of peace began to take hold.

Having experienced multiple losses by this time, I often found myself thinking about past losses. It's something that doesn't automatically disappear from one's mind.

A year later, I was pregnant again. This time, everything felt different—in the best possible way. The ultrasound was clear, and week after week, we received nothing but good news: The baby was healthy and growing beautifully. When we found out the sex early, we were overjoyed—another girl! We named her Angelina, and from that moment on, she became the center of our world.

We threw a baby shower filled with soft pinks, tiny bows, and sweet treats ready to bring a new little girl into the world. Her nursery came to life with delicate butterflies, plush animals, and the name *Angelina* spelled out in pastel-colored hearts above her crib. We imagined her nestled in that room, wrapped in lace blankets, surrounded by love and laughter.

But as my due date came and went, and then another week passed, concern began to creep in. I was now two weeks overdue, and the doctors scheduled an ultrasound to check in on our little one.

I remember lying on the table, the familiar buzz of anticipation humming through me as the technician moved the wand across my belly. She studied the screen for a long moment, then looked up and asked, "Do you know the sex of the baby?"

"Of course," I said with a smile. "It's a girl—Angelina."

She glanced back at the monitor and then turned it toward us. Her expression was calm but amused. "Well... take a look here. You're actually having a boy."

For a moment, the world tilted. A boy?

Then came the laughter—startled and joyful. The disbelief melted into wide-eyed wonder. Just like that, everything we had imagined shifted from butterflies to dinosaurs, from soft pastels to bold, adventurous colors, from fairy tales to toy trains and rocket ships.

That night, we stood in the nursery, gazing up at the hearts above the crib that spelled out *Angelina* and felt an overwhelming sense of awe. We hadn't lost a dream; we had gained a new one. A beautiful, unexpected one. A boy. Our son. And somehow, that surprise made the love even bigger.

Our son was born on St. Patrick's Day, a day already filled with luck and celebration. He arrived with his beautiful blue eyes and a spark of joyful energy, as if he brought his own little pot of gold into our lives. We were grateful for our two beautiful children, born on two important holidays that honored both our predominantly Italian and Irish heritages. Coincidence they were born on two fun family days? I don't think so. With our little family of four, we created joyful and exciting memories, like visiting the family cabin in the summer and letting them connect with the other families like I once had when I was younger.

Over the years, the longing to expand our family didn't fade. We continued to hope for a third child, holding on to the dream with quiet persistence. It wasn't just about expanding our family; it was about the love we still had to give, the space in our hearts that remained open. But that dream was not going to come true. I experienced five more miscarriages after our son Joshua was born.

This time, I kept the grief to myself. By now, we'd learned to wait to share the exciting news until we passed the four-month mark and kept a few of these losses to ourselves to work through together. Each one felt a little more distant, a little more numbing. We held off the excitement in order to break the impact of the disappointment. After a while, we came to terms with the fact that we were lucky to have our two beautiful children. The four of us. And though the sadness never fully left, I learned how to navigate through it, to keep moving forward.

Through this journey, I found my experience gave me the strength to help others who had gone through similar pain. I realized even in the darkest of times, there is a way to heal, and sometimes, the greatest gift we can give is simply being there for each other.

EMOTIONAL FLEXIBILITY— A QUIET STRENGTH

Emotional Flexibility is the ability to experience, regulate, and adapt to a range of emotions in a healthy, grounded way. It's not about denying pain or constantly striving to stay positive; it's about meeting each moment as it is, feeling it fully, and shifting when needed.

Emotions come in waves. We ride the highs, we dip into the lows, and sometimes we feel like we're barely staying afloat. For me, navigating through these many miscarriages in between and after having two beautiful healthy children was one of those seasons where the waves just kept coming. Grief, hope, fear, guilt, exhaustion—all crashing at once. Some days, I couldn't even tell which way was up. My husband and I navigated through this together, many times not sharing even with others but partnering to support each other.

What I learned during that time—slowly, painfully, and imperfectly—is the way we handle our emotions can deeply shape our peace. I'll be honest. I didn't always handle it well. But that's okay. Emotional Flexibility isn't about perfection. It's about practicing awareness—noticing what you're feeling in the moment without trying to numb or escape; acceptance—giving yourself permission to feel those emotions without judgment; adjustment—learning how to shift your response, knowing not every moment needs the same emotional posture; and alignment—choosing to move through your emotions in a way that reflects your values even when it's hard.

When we start tuning into our emotional world, we begin to notice how we show up in life. That awareness can be uncomfortable, especially in seasons of grief or uncertainty, but it's what allows us to grow. It stretches us. It helps us heal.

And growth? It doesn't always look graceful. Sometimes it looks like crying in your car. Sometimes it looks like showing up even if you don't want to. Sometimes it looks like choosing peace when your heart feels like a battlefield.

That's Emotional Flexibility. Quiet. Honest. Real. One of the most powerful tools we can carry with us in this messy, beautiful journey of being human.

And I'll be the first to say—I'm still working on it. I haven't mastered Emotional Flexibility by any means, but I'm a whole lot more aware of it now. I'm also my own worst critic. Just yesterday, on a team call, I caught myself reacting to frustrating news. It wasn't terrible, but afterward, I paused and thought, *"I could've responded differently."* And that pause? That reflection? That was Emotional Flexibility in action. Not perfect but present, with awareness and adjustment.

EVOLVING THROUGH THE SEASONS

Emotional Flexibility begins in childhood, often without even realizing it. It doesn't come from a big, obvious lesson. It happens in those small, raw moments when we're told "no," or when we feel left out, and somehow—eventually—we find a way to be okay again. I think back to the way things felt through the eyes of being a young, curious kid. There was a big age gap between me and my sister, and the same with my cousins, who felt more like lots of older brothers and sisters. Then there was my extended

Russian River summer family that was a wide array of ages—this beautiful, blended community that became a second home.

As the youngest, I often felt like the odd one out. I'm not sure if it was intentional—or maybe it was, since I was probably the little "annoying" one, always asking questions and trying to keep up—but either way, those moments shaped me. They tuned me into my own emotions early on, and, more importantly, made me deeply aware of how others around me were feeling from a young age. It made me a tougher kid, sure, but also a more compassionate one. Strange to say, but it helped me shape my Emotional Flexibility at times for myself and for others around me.

One summer afternoon in Rio Nido, all the older kids were heading off to J's Amusement Park. It was a big deal—the kind of outing that had been talked about for days. J's Amusement Park was *the* coolest place ever when your typical summer days are spent wandering through the redwoods, hanging out at the local pool, and venturing off to the river. It felt like it was hidden in the trees, like a secret just for kids who were finally big enough. The whole place smelled like popcorn and hot pavement with waterslides, and you could hear the rides squeaking and kids screaming from down the road before you even got inside. I was probably five, maybe younger, and I wanted so badly to go. But I was too small, too young. Not this time.

Standing in the gravel driveway at our cabin, I watched them pile into the car, laughter already bubbling before they'd even pulled away. I felt my throat tighten, the heat of tears rising before I even fully understood why. It wasn't just about the amusement park. It was about not being big enough, not being chosen, not being a part of *it*—whatever *it* was—that the older kids got to have.

At that moment, I cried. I sulked. I probably stomped around a little. But eventually, someone—I think it was my Mom—pulled out a popsicle and sat down with me on the porch steps. No one tried to fix the feeling or pretend it wasn't there. She just sat with me in it.

Somehow, I softened. I found my way back to curiosity. I started making a game with rocks in the dirt. I let the sun warm my shoulders again.

That was Emotional Flexibility. I didn't have a name for it then. But I was learning, in that quiet way kids do: *It's okay to feel disappointed. It's okay to be sad.* And also—*the world doesn't end here. Something else always comes.*

It's a lesson I've had to re-learn many times since. But it started on that porch step in Rio Nido, with a red popsicle and a heart just beginning to stretch wide enough to hold both sadness and hope.

Knowing my feelings and how I secretly felt, I started to notice when someone else looked left out, unsure, or small in a space that felt too big for them. That awareness stuck with me. Growing up around my mom—one of the kindest, most caring women you could ever meet—only strengthened it. She showed me what it meant to lead with kindness. And living in a bustling, beautifully diverse city deepened that understanding even more. I learned everyone carries something—something you can't always see—and sometimes, just noticing can make all the difference.

Because of those early experiences many of us navigate, I naturally became the one who would step in. I'd defend a friend, offer a hand, stand beside someone who didn't have a strong friend beside them yet—and help them feel seen. Even at a young age, I knew what it felt like to be on the outside, and I didn't want anyone else to feel that way if I could help it.

What's beautiful is that many of the people I've drawn close to—whether childhood friends, adult friendships, or even work relationships—have naturally aligned with those same core values of inclusion. I think about those Russian River summers as a young child, where there were no real cliques, no divisions, just families spending weekends or summers together, surrounded by redwoods, laughter, ups and downs in life and having this Community. It was like we were dropped in another world for the summer. Kids were welcomed into the fold no matter where they came from, with no judgment. We all developed our sense of Emotional Flexibility growing up together. Seeing so many friends navigate their own challenges made an imprint on me.

Oh, and when I got older, I finally made it to J's Amusement Park—the ultimate thrill at the end of a dirt road. We raced go-karts like we were in the Indy 500, flipped upside down on Round-Up with our stomachs in our throats, and somehow lived to tell the tale after riding the rickety MAD MOUSE roller coaster that felt like it was held together with hope and a rusty screw. Every time we hit a turn, I was *sure* one rogue bolt was going to pop off, send us flying through the air, and launch us straight into the gravel below. And yet, we loved every second of it.

BENDING NOT BREAKING

As you have figured out by now I was an observer. I would watch those around me navigate challenges, taking note, admiring the way things had been handled, and reflecting back when similar moments would arise. Those moments molded me and became part of my foundation and evolved, carrying me through the toughest times in my life. And without a doubt, those moments from childhood to becoming a teen to an adult have also helped shape my amazing friends and now their children as well.

Mental Fortitude and Emotional Flexibility are two parts of the same strength. Fortitude helps us push through pain, stay focused, and keep going. Flexibility allows us to soften when we need to, to feel the hard things without being consumed by them. One without the other can leave us stuck—either too rigid or too unmoored. But together, they create real resilience, the kind that bends but doesn't break. I've found that my ability to persevere through life's hardest moments—grief, anxiety, uncertainty—has always been tied to my ability to let myself feel, pause, and adapt. That balance is where healing happens.

When Mental Fortitude and Emotional Flexibility are supported by a strong Community, we don't just survive—we grow, heal, and move forward with deeper strength than we ever imagined. Everything expands. We stop carrying it all alone. Opening up, asking for help, allowing others in—it multiplies our strength. Community doesn't fix the pain, but it holds space for it, offers perspective, and reminds us we're not alone.

Lori and Josh, then

Lori and Josh, now

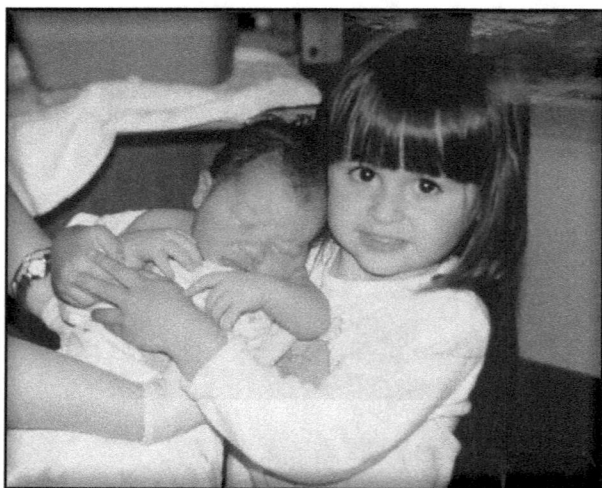

Gianna with Baby Josh

CHAPTER 6

COMMUNITY STRENGTH

Some of the most impactful friendships in my life
came in the form of two remarkable women—
both named Michelle. I often refer to them as "The
Michelles," a nickname that barely scratches the
surface of the strength, wisdom, and support they've
brought into my world. They didn't know it at the
time, but they were quietly transforming my life.

Our paths first crossed casually, chatting on the
sidelines of countless soccer games while our boys
played on the same fields, weekend after weekend. At
the time, they had no idea about my past—especially
the trauma of my kidnapping. That wasn't something
I opened up about until years later. But even without

knowing the full story, they instinctively showed up for me in ways I hadn't even realized I needed.

Bonding over a shared passion for health and wellness, we began spending our weekend mornings walking and hiking together. What started as simple exercise quickly grew into something much more meaningful—an ongoing ritual that offered space for connection, healing, and growth. Those hikes became our mini therapy sessions, filled with laughter, honest conversation, emotional release, and mutual support. Michelle M., a Clinical Psychologist, had just opened her own practice in our community. It is now very apparent her career fits her well—helping others. With a gift for listening and values that mirrored my own, our friendship felt effortless and grounding. Michelle H. radiated warmth and compassion. She has the kind of presence that makes you feel truly seen—someone who listens with her whole heart.

A true sense of Community blossomed with every hike we shared. Our conversations never ran dry. We talked about everything—motherhood, life's curveballs, personal wins both big and small. What we shared was more than companionship—it was a lifeline. We saw each other clearly, held space for one another's truths, and reminded each other to keep showing up for ourselves, too.

Our hikes became sacred rituals, always ending at a favorite coffee shop, where the comfort of caffeine met the comfort of connection.

I've been blessed with many incredible women throughout my life, especially during my time in Arizona—but these two? They helped me rediscover my strength. They reminded me of the healing power of friendship and the quiet magic of walking beside someone, both literally and figuratively, through life.

Alongside those rich in-person connections, I was also growing in quieter ways. I began diving into podcasts, drawn to stories and voices that challenged and expanded me. Each episode was like a doorway—offering new ways to think, to heal, to understand. One show in particular, which I mentioned back in Chapter 4, is *The School of Greatness* with Lewis Howes. There was something in it that felt personal as if the stories were speaking directly to me. Whether I was walking, driving, or folding laundry, I'd find myself immersed in stories of resilience—people who had turned pain into purpose, hardship into healing. Their journeys lit something inside of me. They reminded me that struggle wasn't the end of the story, it could be the beginning of something meaningful.

Then, something unexpected happened—I had the chance to attend an event connected to *The School of Greatness* and meet some of the very voices who had inspired me through my hardest moments and helped lay the foundation for my success. These weren't just names behind a podcast—they were real people whose words had shifted how I saw myself and what I believed was possible. The opportunity felt surreal, like a bridge between the inner transformation I had been working on and the outer world I was finally ready to step into. Their impactful messages fueled my fire, pushing me to challenge myself both personally and professionally, driving me toward goals I hadn't even known were within reach. My hour-long ride to work became a ritual, each podcast leaving me fired up and energized to crush the day ahead.

Without hesitation, I asked the Michelles if they'd come with me. And without hesitation, they said yes. That's who they are—loyal, uplifting, and always ready to stand beside someone chasing something meaningful but also genuinely excited to see and experience what this was all about. Our bond gave each of us the confidence to try something new. Planning the trip sparked a new kind of joy—an anticipation that reached beyond our usual hikes and coffee dates. This wasn't just about an event. It was about stepping into something greater, together. And that made it even more powerful. My journey no longer felt like mine alone. It was something shared—built on trust, love, and the kind of friendship that makes transformation possible.

MAKING TIME FOR GROWTH

One of the most powerful things you can do for your growth personally, professionally, and spiritually is to build a strong Community around you. Whether it's the people you meet at self-development summits, your local bookclub or gym, or even online, these connections are game-changers. You're stepping into a space filled with growth-minded individuals who genuinely want to see you thrive. These aren't just surface-level encounters. When you show up fully, they can evolve into accountability partnerships, lasting friendships, or unexpected opportunities. The right conversation might spark a new habit, introduce a life-changing book, or open the door to a venture you hadn't imagined. These micro-communities—

whether emotional, intellectual, or practical—each play a vital role in your growth and transformation.

Having people around you with different experiences brings fresh perspectives. Maybe someone from a totally different walk of life will say something that clicks and reframes your whole situation. Others hold space for you during hard times or celebrate your wins when no one else really gets it.

What's even more powerful is when your Community spans different generations. When you're connected to older mentors and younger dreamers, you tap into a beautiful balance of wisdom and curiosity. You learn from those who've walked before you, and you pass your own insight down to those just beginning their journey. That kind of multigenerational support creates deep, lasting impact. Whether you're working on your mindset, health, career, or just trying to stay consistent, Community amplifies your growth. It's like adding wind to your sails. You move faster, stronger, and with more clarity when you're not doing it alone.

And then there are the communities that form around memories—the seasonal chapters of life that quietly shape who you are. For me, one of those was my Russian River summer family I wrote about in Chapter 5.

Every summer, the same families would return, bringing lawn chairs, river floats, summer attire, old stories, and new laughter. It wasn't just a vacation, it was a second life that ran in parallel to the one back home. Kids became teenagers, teenagers grew into young adults, and year after year, we watched each other transform. It was a mix of so many different friends growing up in their own unique ways, yet no one was ever left out. We looked at every kid as part of our summer Community. You wouldn't typically find us bringing our city friends along to visit the summer cabin—this was our unique squad, one that welcomed everyone to embark on a new journey together.

We were always on an adventure. Our parents secretly knew what we were up to, but they never interfered, trusting that we all were on a journey together and would all look out for each other, which was such an important piece of our childhood. We had the opportunity to explore and make mistakes (while still making pretty good choices). We trekked deep among the redwoods, climbing trees like they were part of our endless playground and wandering through old, abandoned houses with that electrifying mix of fear and excitement buzzing in our chests. There were endless tales about the legendary Garlic House—that mysterious spot that was half dare, half warning with garlic hanging from the high eerie ceiling—and the memorable sight of the man with the staff standing silently as we gallivanted through the canyons by night, always in pairs. Night hikes often turned into impromptu games of hide and seek in the cemetery. We pushed our limits, challenged our courage, and revelled in those wild, silly moments that cemented our bonds.

We didn't know it at the time, but we were building something deep: our confidence, curiosity, and bravery were all taking root in these shared moments. We built memories that have stayed with us, a reminder we were all accepted and ready for new journeys together.

Our parents were also building their friendships and bonds with the other parents. The ladies would meet up at the local pool every day by 11 a.m. to get their set seating and hang with their circle of friends, catching up on the latest news, swapping the most recent novels, and building their own Community of summer friends, while the dads did the same around the card tables playing serious games of Pedro. The parents were just as excited to open up the cabin for the summer and spend their days with their summer friends.

Separate from my Russian River Family, back in the city, Maria, Tara, and I grew up together, watching each other go through all kinds of challenges—loss of loved ones, relationship drama, changing into young adults, and finding ourselves. Yet even as life took us in different directions, we always stayed connected. We made new friends, stepped into new spaces, but our bond never wavered. We've always been there in the background for each other, offering quiet support, fierce loyalty, and a deep understanding only time can forge.

That's the power of Community. It's not just the people who cheer for your wins, but those who walk beside you through every chapter—listening, showing up, and growing with you.

When we moved to Arizona, some of those deep-rooted friendships stayed remarkably intact. Despite the distance, all it took was a single call to pick up right where we left off. That kind of connection—the kind that weathers time and silence without losing its depth—is the most meaningful to me. I'm endlessly grateful for those lasting bonds, especially the ones formed in childhood and during my Russian River days. They hold a unique kind of magic that time or space can't touch.

This was the beginning of Community for me. I didn't fully understand it then, but those early relationships quietly laid the foundation for everything that came after.

SUMMIT OF GREATNESS

After that conversation with the Michelles about taking a trip to Columbus, Ohio, for the Summit of Greatness, I came home inspired and excited and immediately started planning. Once again my husband was by my side supporting me to go, after we got through the discussion that it wasn't a cult. He, too, was surprised by my impulse to make it happen, but he was there to support and cheer me on to help me hit my goals and thrive.

I had never been to Columbus before, but that didn't matter. The Michelles and I were determined to go, and we always pushed each other to step out of the norm. At that point in my life, I was craving growth and already feeling the impact of the Summit through Lewis Howes' podcast. Even just listening had sparked a creative shift in me, especially at work.

Our company was growing fast—almost too fast to keep up—but I was committed to not falling behind and making an impact. It wasn't just a job to me; I was invested to help my work family grow. I wanted to keep evolving in my role, and the tools and insights from the podcast helped me unlock new ideas and add value in ways I hadn't imagined. That growth led to a promotion I never thought I'd reach, and by the time I was booking my trip to the Summit, I knew I had to find a way to thank Lewis in person for the impact he'd had on my journey.

From the moment I arrived, I made it my mission to experience everything the event had to offer. I signed up for every micro-event, like the early morning workouts where I met so many incredible people and pushed myself to speak to as many attendees as I could. I wanted to fully immerse myself in the experience. Normally, I'm more reserved around strangers, but something about that space energized me. I came out of my shell in a way I never had before. Surrounded by people who were just as hungry for growth, I opened up, and it paid off. I met amazing individuals from all over the world—some who would become close friends, distant cheerleaders reaching out from time to time, and even accountability partners. That first weekend turned out to be one of the most transformative experiences of my life.

I even had the chance to meet Lewis in person and share how much his podcast had impacted me. His response—a genuine, heartfelt hug, a high five, and encouragement to keep climbing, congratulating me for the work I had put in—meant everything to me in that moment. It was a simple gesture, but it felt like a celebration of how far I had come.

That first Summit sparked the beginning of what became an annual tradition: a time each year to learn, set bold, new goals, and fuel my growth. Life, like I know it is for so many of you, is non-stop—between raising little ones, managing work and finances, supporting others, and trying to pour into ourselves, it's easy to put our own growth on the back burner. But after that first time, I made a promise to prioritize *me*—so I could be even more present, impactful, and energized for everyone else.

Each year, I would return with an even bigger squad by my side—always a little more confident, always more fired up. The Michelles and I formed powerful new connections and always came home feeling fueled and focused. We set bold goals, held each other accountable, and made it our mission every year to become even greater than the year before.

The Community I've built through the Summit of Greatness has surrounded me with some of the most inspiring and uplifting individuals I've ever met. If you've attended the Summit—whether in its early years in Columbus, Ohio, or more recently in Los Angeles—there's a good chance you've come across my original "Summit Squad." They were the ones who set the tone for what this experience would mean to me year after year.

First, there's the incredible Kimberly Karr, co-founder of Digital4Good. She's dedicated her life to empowering students, educators, and communities through digital safety and promoting positive online interactions. Kim is the real deal—an absolute force of energy who has this amazing ability to draw people out of their shells. Her determination and warmth are contagious, and she makes everyone feel like they belong.

Then there's Desiree Maya—author, host of the *Born Unbreakable* podcast, and a transformational coach who lives what she teaches. She's fierce, always evolving, and constantly encouraging those around her to step into their own growth and transformation.

Brenden Kumarasamy, the voice behind the YouTube Channel *MasterTalk* podcast, has been instrumental in helping me strengthen my public speaking skills, and it has been an inspiration to see him evolve year after year.

And DJ Cardenas—our conversations about leadership left a lasting impression on me and helped spark a meaningful connection as I was stepping into an even stronger version of myself as a leader.

Then there's Daya Rebolledo. One morning, during a group run before the Summit of Greatness officially kicked off, I struck up a conversation with a sweet soul named Daya. As we kept pace with the group, we began swapping stories about our journeys. Daya shared she had recently been laid off from a major payments company and was facing a lot of uncertainty about what was next. Despite the fear and unknowns, she spoke with so much heart about her true passion: stepping into the world of speaking and inspiring others. We instantly clicked. I remember us talking about how taking chances can be terrifying, but that sometimes the biggest growth comes from the biggest leaps, and how powerful it is to choose courage, even when the future feels unclear.

And that's just a glimpse.

Every year at Summit, you meet people who feel like soul connections—the ones who don't just align with your goals, but who also inspire you to dream even bigger. Summit is about Community, lifting each other up, cheering each other on, and creating a space where growth feels possible for everyone.

Each year, I walk into the Summit with a new goal—sometimes small, sometimes scary but always meaningful. What may seem basic to others has felt monumental to me. *Year One:* Earn a promotion. *Year Two:* Buy a new car. *Year Three:* Purchase a new home and bring my daughter along to help her start building her own Summit Community. *Year Four:* Begin writing my book and sharing my story. And now, heading into Year Five this September with my sister Lisa by my side, I can't wait to reconnect with my Summit family, catch up on their journeys, and set the next intention for what's to come.

That's the true magic of this Community. It's not about setting massive goals just for the sake of it. It's about committing to your growth, year after year, and showing up for yourself in ways you never thought possible. Even if you don't achieve every goal exactly as you planned, it's still a success. Every step forward, every effort made, is progress. Simply moving toward a new path is an achievement in itself.

Even if an event like the Summit of Greatness isn't possible right now, there are still so many ways to build a meaningful Community right where you are. Host a small coffee meetup, start a book club, or join local events and volunteer opportunities. Don't overlook your workplace. Participating in team outings, wellness challenges, or interest-based groups can create unexpected and valuable connections. Online spaces like virtual accountability groups or forums also offer deep support. Whether it's a walk with a neighbor or a goal-setting night with friends, Community begins with intention—and showing up.

By tapping into your Mental Fortitude and Emotional Flexibility, you can lean into Community and begin to face the fears that once held you back. Because if you do... you'll discover strength you didn't know you had, connections that lift you higher, and a version of yourself that's been waiting to rise just like a Phoenix.

COURAGE IN COMMUNITY

This memoir begins with what has become one of the most profound truths in my life: healing and growth aren't meant to be done alone. As time passed, and I reflected on the many conversations I'd shared with the Michelles during our long hikes and coffee outings—and with the incredible women I'm lucky to call lifelong friends even from a distance, and my strong friendships at work—I began to notice a shift in myself. I was becoming more at ease with showing up as my full self. I wasn't hiding my thoughts. I wasn't keeping my guard up. For the first time, I was letting people in, and it felt like a quiet kind of freedom.

In moments where my story could serve a purpose or bring comfort to someone else, I started choosing courage. I had pushed past the discomfort to speak honestly. I'll never forget when a team member opened up to me with a story very close to mine and leaned on me for support once I opened up to share my story. It gave me the chance to offer more than support; I could offer understanding. That's when I realized another important truth: Community isn't just about being held; it's about holding others, too.

The Michelles at Summit in Ohio

Lori thanking Lewis

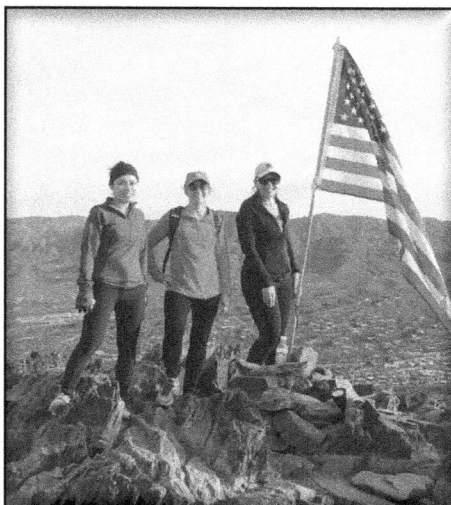

Lori with Michelles on a hike

Lori and Tara

Lori and Maria

CHAPTER 7

OVERCOMING FEAR AND MOVING FORWARD

Fear and I have been old companions for as long as I can remember—a silent shadow trailing my every step, always near enough I could feel its breath on the back of my neck. As a child, nothing unsettled me more than the thought of speaking aloud in front of others. The mere idea of standing at the front of the classroom, dozens of eyes pinned to me, made my chest tighten as if invisible hands were squeezing the air from my lungs. It wasn't just nerves; it was a full-body paralysis, a battle between wanting to disappear and knowing I couldn't.

I can't pinpoint the exact moment fear rooted itself so deeply in me. Was it those early, humiliating stumbles—the wrong answers blurted out in class, the hot flush of embarrassment creeping up my neck as classmates snickered? Maybe. What I do remember is the way those moments taught me to retreat inward, to live inside my head, analyzing, second-guessing, trying to solve the riddle of how to be invisible and perfect all at once.

Back then, kids didn't really talk about their fears or insecurities the way they seem to now. There were no safe spaces online, no candid posts or encouraging messages just a swipe away. Vulnerability wasn't fashionable; it felt dangerous. You carried your doubts in silence, hoping no one could see how heavy they had become.

But life, with its relentless wisdom, has a way of cornering you, pushing you toward the very things you fear most, over and over again. For me, stepping into leadership roles wasn't a gradual, comfortable choice; it felt more like a collision. It wasn't that I lacked the ability; I had what it took. Deep down, I knew I was capable, that I possessed the heart, instincts, and resilience to rise to the challenge. Of course, I was still learning with each new role I took on, stumbling at times, growing, and drawing inspiration from the leaders I had admired over the many years. Three mentors who stand out most to me were three strong women: Mary Ann, Jocelyne, and Heidi. Each of them played a powerful role in shaping my journey, offering not just guidance but living examples of strength, wisdom, and integrity. I learned so much from observing how they led, how they carried themselves, and how they consistently lifted up those around them. The foundation had been laid by these inspiring leaders—I just had to trust it and continue building upon it as I moved forward.

Somewhere along the way, I realized my ideas and my voice had value. I wasn't that scared little girl anymore, fumbling for the right words and fearing the spotlight. As an adult, I knew my thoughts could help shape teams, guide decisions, and contribute to something bigger than myself. The real challenge wasn't finding the words; it was quieting the small, trembling voice of *Little Lori* in my head, the one still whispering doubts from old wounds. I had to learn to push past her, to reassure her, and then move forward with the confidence that the woman I had become had something worth saying.

The transformation wasn't neat, and it certainly wasn't instant. It was slow, uneven, and messy at times early on in my career—a process full of moments of hesitation and learning. Progress came one shaky step at a time, inching forward, falling back, dusting myself off, and pushing on. It meant trusting myself, even when it felt uncomfortable and unfamiliar. If I wanted to build the career and life I envisioned, I had to make a choice: continue hiding in the shadows or step into the light, no matter how vulnerable it made me feel.

That's the real journey—not erasing fear, but standing toe-to-toe with it. Finding your voice when doubt tries to drown it out. Moving forward anyway, even when your whole body trembles.

One moment stands out in my memory, so vivid it could have happened yesterday. I was invited to a major event with the top executives and leaders from across my company. I felt a deep, swelling pride— proud to have earned a seat at that table—but just beneath that pride was raw, unshakable terror. These leaders knew my name. They knew my work. But they hadn't met *me* in person. This was it—my first impression. My moment.

As I stood up to speak, my heart pounded so hard it thundered in my ears. I half-expected everyone in the room to hear it. I could feel the heat rushing to my face—I turned bright red, fully aware my nervousness was on display for everyone to see. Worst-case scenarios flashed through my mind—what if I stumbled? What if I forgot my words? But somehow, despite it all, I found my footing. I spoke. I stood. And that day, I learned a truth I would carry with me: Courage isn't about the absence of fear; it's about choosing to stand and speak despite it.

If you're wondering how it went, it was okay. Not perfect. I still stumbled through a few too many "ums" and spoke a little too fast, rushing to get to the end. But I didn't give up. I didn't hide. Instead, I got serious about getting better. I began preparing more thoughtfully, sometimes recording myself so I could review and refine my delivery. I realized growth wasn't about perfection; it was about persistence, about reclaiming my voice piece by piece.

The fear didn't disappear overnight. Sometimes, it still lingers at the edges. But once I made the decision to *invest* in myself and welcomed the discomfort that came with growth, everything began to shift. I started asking trusted colleagues for feedback after presentations, choosing to see their insights as gifts rather than judgments. I leaned into learning, turning to resources in my Community like my friend Brenden from *MasterTalk* on YouTube, finding practical ways to strengthen my skills and build new habits.

Every small step forward mattered. Every ounce of effort added up.

I conquered it. Not because the fear disappeared, but because I proved to myself I could rise above it.

And that's the kind of victory no one can ever take away.

STEPPING INTO YOUR FEARS

Fear is a universal experience—a thread woven through every human life, no matter how different our paths may seem. We fear the psychological: failure, rejection, and judgment. We fear not being enough, losing what we love, or facing the unknown. Even success, with all its promises, can spark its own brand of anxiety, bringing the fear of pressure, expectation, and being exposed in ways we're not ready for.

Then there are the moments when fear isn't conceptual or social; it's physical and immediate, like being forced at gunpoint into my own car. In that moment, fear wasn't an emotion; it was a pulse, a tightness in my chest, a rush of survival instincts pressing against the sheer terror of what might come next. That kind of fear bypasses thought; it just *is*. It stays with you, stored in your body long after the danger passes.

As I stepped into leadership roles during my career, speaking up became non-negotiable. It wasn't about preference anymore; it was a necessity. If I wanted to lead, to inspire, to contribute meaningfully, I had to find my voice. It wasn't that I lacked insight or ideas; I knew I was capable. But the old fear, the one I had carried since childhood, still clung tightly.

The breakthrough didn't happen overnight. It came slowly, with each moment I chose to speak despite the fear sitting beside me. I learned to carry it, to walk with it, instead of letting it paralyze me. I began to see that fear didn't have to define or control me anymore. It could be acknowledged—without being obeyed.

And yet, there was another kind of fear shaping my life: the fear embedded in my deep desire to please others. For much of my life, I worked hard to make sure everyone around me felt comfortable and supported. I believed if I could keep the peace, maybe I could avoid the pain of conflict or disappointment.

My desire to help, to fix, to smooth things over wasn't manipulation; it came from a place of genuine care. But beneath it lived fear. Fear that if I didn't make others happy, they might not like me. Or worse—they might leave.

This made me feel like I had to put everyone's needs above my own. I became the mediator, the steady one, the person everyone could depend on, but often at the cost of my own well-being. Sometimes, I stood up for myself, sure, but it wasn't always easy. The pressure to make everyone happy was a constant tug-of-war inside me.

In recent years, I took a personality test that revealed something I didn't want to admit: I had strong people-pleasing tendencies. My first reaction was frustration. *Am I really a people pleaser?* I didn't think of myself that way. I didn't *look* like one. But the more I reflected, the more I realized the truth. I had spent years prioritizing others' comfort out of fear. Fear of conflict. Fear of rejection. Fear of being perceived as not enough.

That revelation hit hard, but it also opened the door to real growth. I began to understand just how much I had been sacrificing my own needs and boundaries. I started seeing that my worth wasn't tied to others' approval. It was okay to say no. It was okay to have limits. I didn't need to be everything for everyone. And I didn't need to do it all alone.

This shift was gradual. My role at work was expanding, my workload growing, and the expectations I had once willingly taken on were becoming unsustainable. From a young age, I had operated with a customer-service mindset—my "customers" being my colleagues, team, and anyone who needed support. I had trained everyone to expect instant replies, immediate help, and constant availability.

But there was only one Lori.

I had to redefine what helpfulness looked like. Not because I cared less, but because I physically and emotionally couldn't continue at that pace. I had to learn to pause, prioritize, and give myself grace. I had to let go of the guilt that surfaced when I couldn't meet everyone's needs at once. And that meant doing something terrifying—setting boundaries.

It also meant stepping a little outside my comfort zone. Not dramatically, but in those quiet, powerful choices, I had to trust my instincts, to say what I truly thought, to choose authenticity over perfection. That's when I began to tap into the resilient, brave version of myself—the part that had always been there, quietly building strength in the background.

What I've learned is fear's true antidote isn't bravado or pretending it doesn't exist. It's connection. It's the willingness to reach out and say, *I'm scared,* and let someone respond with, *Me, too.* Fear loses its power when it's brought into the light—spoken aloud in the company of those who understand. These are people who listen without judgment, who remind you courage isn't about being fearless; it's about choosing to move forward, even when your legs shake.

Community is where fear softens. In honest conversations. In knowing glances. In texts that say, *You've got this.* It's leaning on someone else's strength when your own feels shaky. It's realizing bravery isn't a solo act. True bravery often happens in small, unseen moments—when someone's belief in us fuels the belief we haven't yet found in ourselves.

There were many times in my life when fear nearly swallowed me whole. But connection saved me. A mentor's encouragement. A friend's steady presence. A team's belief in my ideas. Each gesture chipped away at the walls I'd built around myself.

Today, fear still visits me. But I no longer see it as a sign that I'm not ready. I see it as an invitation. A reminder that something meaningful is ahead. And I remember I don't have to face it alone. Fear may walk with me, but it no longer leads. Because I've learned connection is stronger than fear. And that's what gives me the courage to keep going.

FROM FEAR TO GROWTH

While fear may never fully vanish, the way we respond to it can change everything. For years, I pushed through the fear from that day in 2011. Eventually, it began to feel like a distant nightmare from childhood—fuzzy around the edges, something I could recall without fully reliving. The image would flicker into my mind and then drift away, like a boat just visible on the horizon but never docking again. Even the bandana—once a trigger that could send my body into panic—lost its grip. The memory didn't disappear, but it no longer had power over me.

When we stop trying to outrun fear and instead turn toward it with curiosity, we often find it points us directly toward the areas of our greatest growth. Fear shines a spotlight on the places where we care the most, where something important is at stake. Learning to work with fear, rather than against it, is a lifelong practice, but it's a practice that can completely transform the way we live.

One of the first and most powerful solutions for fear is simply naming it. Fear thrives in the unknown. It grows larger and more menacing when it stays vague and shadowy. But when we name it, when we say, I am afraid of failing, or I am afraid of being judged, we strip it of some of its power. Suddenly, it's no longer a shapeless dread; it's something we can look at clearly. Naming fear turns it from a monster into a challenge. And challenges, unlike monsters, can be prepared for and overcome.

Take a moment right now—pause wherever you are reading this—and think about one fear that has been lingering quietly in the back of your mind. Maybe it's a fear tied to your career, your relationships, your dreams, or simply the next step you've been too hesitant to take. Name it. Give it words. Write it down. You don't have to solve it today, but by identifying it, you are already beginning to change your relationship with it. You are showing yourself that you are willing to face it, rather than be silently ruled by it.

Another crucial piece is self-compassion. Fear often triggers a harsh inner critic—that voice saying you're weak for being scared or foolish for wanting more. But responding to fear with judgment only deepens its roots. True strength comes from learning to greet fear with gentleness. Of course you're scared. This matters to you. This is new. This is brave. When we speak to ourselves with the same kindness we would offer a struggling friend, we give ourselves permission to move through fear rather than getting stuck inside it.

Preparation and small steps are practical, tangible ways to face fear. Fear thrives on the unknown, but preparation builds familiarity. If public speaking terrifies you, start by practicing in front of a trusted friend. If change paralyzes you, break the transition down into tiny steps you can actually manage. Action creates momentum, and momentum slowly starves fear of its hold. You don't have to leap the entire mountain in a single bound; often, it's the small, steady steps that create the most lasting courage.

Perhaps the most important solution of all is connection, Community. Fear isolates. It tricks us into believing we are the only ones struggling, the only ones trembling behind the scenes. But the truth is, every single person carries fear at some point, often about the very same things we are scared to admit. Sharing our fears in safe, trusted spaces defangs them. Speaking our fears aloud to people who hold them tenderly—friends, mentors, therapists, communities—reminds us we are not strange or broken for feeling afraid. We are human. And humans are wired for connection, for support, for encouragement when the road feels long.

Building a support system isn't just helpful; it's essential. We need people who remind us of who we are when fear tries to make us forget. We need the ones who say, *I see your fear and I believe in you anyway.* Sometimes, the courage we need isn't found inside ourselves at first; it's borrowed from the people who love us until we can build it up in our own hearts.

Reframing fear can also make an enormous difference. What if fear isn't a stop sign? What if it's a green light, signaling you're about to step into a part of your life that matters? What if fear is a reminder you're expanding, growing, reaching beyond what you once thought possible? Viewing fear as a sign of importance rather than a warning of doom changes the entire emotional equation. Instead of seeing fear as the enemy, we can see it as evidence that we're alive, paying attention, and standing at the edge of something worthwhile.

Finally, embracing resilience, the understanding that setbacks are part of growth, softens the sharp edges of fear. You will stumble. You will feel discomfort. You will question yourself. But resilience whispers, *You can get back up again and again,* and each time you do, fear loses a little more of its control over you.

The journey with fear isn't about eliminating it; it's about changing your relationship with it. Fear will still knock on your door from time to time, but you'll recognize it now. You'll know its tricks. You'll greet it with curiosity, kindness, and the fierce strength of Community beside you. And you'll move forward anyway, not because you aren't afraid, but because what's waiting for you on the other side is too important to miss.

By leaning into discomfort and taking decisive action, I came to understand that courage isn't the absence of fear but the willingness to move forward despite it. Fear has become a powerful source of empowerment. Each step, each moment of vulnerability, has laid the groundwork for a stronger, more resilient version of myself. True strength isn't about avoiding fear; it's about harnessing it as fuel to propel me forward. Through this journey, I forged Titanium Strength—unyielding and steadfast, shaped by my courage to face my fears head-on and rise above them. My goal isn't perfection but growth and continual evolution toward the best version of myself.

CHAPTER 8

EMBRACING THE MESSINESS OF LIFE

L ife doesn't come with a manual, and neither do relationships. We stumble through it all—trying to love, connect, forgive, and grow—while juggling everyday things like the day to day laundry, schedules, and finances, along with miscommunication, grief, joy, and everything in between. Sometimes it's beautiful. Sometimes it's a complete mess. And most of the time, it's both.

Through it all, I often felt like I had to keep everything together to be worthy of love or respect. But it turns out, the most meaningful moments in my life weren't the polished ones; they were the raw, unfiltered ones. The arguments, the breakdowns, the awkward silences, learning to parent the best way I knew at the moment to the then unexpected laughter. The truth is, everyone has their version of chaos.

But life isn't about getting everything right—there is no magic potion for anything—it's about learning to grow in the middle of the mess. I used to think things like self-doubt or procrastination were signs I was failing at being an adult. Yet over time, I began to see them for what they really are: invitations to slow down, reflect, and be honest with myself.

I've second-guessed my worth more times than I can count. I've put off hard conversations and decisions because they felt too heavy or uncomfortable. I've battled insecurities about whether I was "enough"—as a partner, a parent, and a friend. I've spent sleepless nights overthinking things I wish I had said differently or handled better.

But here's what no one tells you when you're younger: These struggles don't disqualify you from living a meaningful life. They shape you for it. They teach you compassion. They show you your edges. And eventually, if you're willing to lean in, they push you to grow.

One of the biggest lessons I've learned—much later than I wish I had—is how to set boundaries. Not as walls to shut people out but as a way to protect the parts of me that were constantly trying to prove, please, and perform. Learning to say "no" without guilt and "yes" with clarity was one of the most freeing things I've ever done. It's these little moments and shifts that we make that create Titanium Strength.

Titanium Strength doesn't come from things going smoothly. It comes from breaking, bending, sometimes saying no, and sometimes even rebuilding. It comes from standing from standing in the mess and still choosing to rise. Life's imperfections demand something deep from us: the grit to keep going (*Mental Fortitude*), the ability to pivot and soften when the path shifts (*Emotional Flexibility*), and the willingness to be held when we can't hold ourselves (*Community*). It wasn't until I was completely broken that I was able to understand and embrace how truly strong I was and to see that strength in those I love the most.

THIS IS US: LOVE, LAUGHTER, AND THE LONG HAUL

As far back as I can remember, I dreamed of finding that perfect partner—my own version of a fairytale love story. I imagined the kind of wedding you see in Disney movies, stitching together pieces of all those magical moments: the sweeping gown, the emotional vows, the deep feeling of being truly seen and chosen.

I think I started manifesting the love of my life the moment I saw his photo. It all began one weekend at my cousin Julie's house. I was just a freshman in high school, the youngest in the mix, and Julie—a few years older—was more than just family. She felt like a second sister. We had grown especially close over the years, spending countless summers together at the Russian River, where we'd stay up late talking, laughing, and dreaming about life. She took me under her wing, brought me along when she went out, and was always by my side when I needed someone the most.

That day, I was sitting on her perfectly made bed in her impeccably spotless room flipping through her high school yearbook when I suddenly stopped. I stared. And I said, half-jokingly but fully serious, *"Dang, this Barbarotto is fine."*

There was something about him I couldn't look away from—maybe it was those strong, sparkling green eyes, or that fly '90s haircut every guy seemed to want back then. And let's be honest, having a last name like *Barbarotto*? That was just plain cool. Whatever it was, something about him grabbed my attention, and it never really let go.

We cracked up, and it became a running joke. Every year, when a new yearbook came out, I'd flip through it just to find his picture. There he was—again. We'd laugh, tease, and move on. It was innocent fun, part of the silly, sweet crushes and banter that made up those teenage years.

What I didn't know back then was that this inside joke would one day turn into something real.

Years later, we started crossing paths through Julie and my cousin Jennine, Julie's lifelong best friend and neighbor. I was mortified the first time I actually met him. I remember the awkwardness, whispering and laughing with my friends, immediately paging Maria to share the story with her, and trying to play it cool. I didn't expect him to even notice me, let alone later be interested. I had always been the girl with tons of guy friends—the wing-girl to all my close guy friends, the buddy—not the one guys crushed on. But there he was, asking for my number as we were all piling into a car, heading out for a group night in San Francisco.

I was so shocked that I could barely speak. My face turned bright red, and all I could manage was to rattle off my beeper number. Yep—this was the '90s. If you had a beeper, you were pretty much the definition of cool.

That one night led to a friendship… then a relationship. There were ups and downs, of course—on-and-off phases, like most young love stories—but eventually years later, it led to marriage. And somehow, through it all, he's still standing beside me today.

Marriage is no cakewalk. It gets messy—frustrating, confusing, even lonely at times. But over the years, we've learned to turn our heads during the hardest moments and refocus on what truly matters: each other, our adult children, and now, our beloved furbabies, who somehow fill this next chapter with even more love, laughter, and resilience. In essence, we've created a titanium-strong partnership.

We've essentially grown up together—learning, unlearning, adapting, and stumbling side by side. The mistakes we made many years ago no longer define us as we grew together. We don't hold them over each other's heads, as we were also growing through these experiences. Instead, we look forward, committed to building the best future we can—together. Now, being married for just over twenty-five years, we know each other's boundaries, passions, and flaws. And we've learned to adjust—not out of duty but out of love, the kind of love that's been tested, shaped, and deepened by experience.

I'm grateful we never walked away or gave up. We chose each other. And we continue to choose each other—every single day. That's what growth looks like in a marriage. That's what letting go and holding on at the same time feels like. This is us becoming a stronger version of ourselves, as a team.

When we hit bumps, it was the steady support of siblings and friends who understood the real, unfiltered parts of marriage, as well as our own parents, who stepped in not to fix us but to remind us that love doesn't always look perfect. Sometimes, it just looks like staying.

This teamwork was also tough and messy for us as parents. We went through so much with the day-to-day logistics of keeping two small humans alive and went through even more feeling the pressure to grow, provide, and do what's right, at least what we thought was right at the moment. The hormones and emotions of raising kids to teenagers in high school and later on to college—it was a lot. If you are a parent, we, as parents, have been through the wringer trying to navigate through it all.

Watching your children move through their highest highs to their deepest lows is one of the hardest parts of parenthood—something no one can truly prepare you for. I don't know a single parent who would say the journey is easy. But this is life. This is us—learning, adjusting, and doing our best to walk alongside them.

WHAT WE BUILD IN SILENCE

Titanium Strength isn't loud. It doesn't always come in the form of raised fists or dramatic victories. Sometimes, it looks like a small boy standing quietly on the sideline, waiting for his name or number to be called.

Our son Joshua was never the biggest kid on the soccer field. He had remarkable footwork and skill, and you could always count on him to set up his teammates for the goal. But as he got older, his height and size were a challenge. At a glance, he didn't seem like much of a threat—small for his age, quiet by nature. Coaches noticed the louder kids, the ones who took up space with boldness, and Josh was easy to overlook. But what they didn't see right away was what he carried inside: a quiet kind of fortitude, the kind that isn't taught but revealed.

Game after game, he suited up. He showed up, even knowing at times he might not play much. He stood there, cleats planted in the grass, heart wide open, waiting to be called in. And in the earlier years, even when he wasn't called in until the last few minutes—or on some days not at all—he kept coming back. Not once did he quit. That's where his Titanium Strength began to take shape. Not in the moments of glory but in the waiting. In the not-giving-up. In the silent promise to himself: *I belong here, even if no one sees it yet.*

But here's the thing about titanium: it's forged under pressure.

Josh adapted. Not by becoming someone else, but by holding tightly to who he was—the kind, patient kid who kept showing up. He didn't grow bitter. Sure, he was disappointed at times. But he still suited up. He still went to every practice, every tournament, giving more of himself each time. He didn't shut down. He stayed hopeful. He stayed open. He leaned into family, into the few meaningful connections that remained. He kept showing up—in his own way, on his own terms.

That's the kind of strength we often don't recognize until much later. The strength that doesn't yell, *Look at me,* but quietly whispers, *I'm still here.*

Titanium Strength is a blend of mental endurance, emotional adaptability, and the deep, often invisible power of connection—especially when it's scarce. Josh didn't become strong because everything went right. He became strong because it didn't, and he kept going anyway.

WHEN SPARKS RETURN AND STRENGTH TAKES ROOT

Gianna reached a major turning point in college—a season full of emotional weight and dramatic change. She'd been moving toward a future that, at first, felt familiar and safe but ultimately wasn't aligned with who she was becoming. It took incredible strength for her to step away—from certain friendships, familiar environments, and long-held expectations—to rediscover herself and find the kind of people who could support her true growth.

As her mom, I was so worried. She was walking through one of her hardest years, and every instinct in me wanted to fix it, to offer a solution, because that's who I've always been: the fixer. But she wasn't having it. She didn't need my fixing. She needed space. My husband and I had to step back; we had to take a seat on the bench. We weren't in the starting five anymore. She was building her own team, and she needed people who could help her take the court on her own terms.

She struggled at first. My husband and I stayed close, offering quiet reassurance: *We're here when you need us.* But this was her moment. Her Titanium Strength was rising. Gradually, she began forming a new circle—people who shared her values, who saw her for the radiant, kind, and courageous person she is. These friendships felt like the kind that last a lifetime. She was seeking the ones who would lift her up, rush to her side when she needed someone to lean on—friends who offered love without judgment. But just as importantly, she wanted to give back—to be that kind of friend in return. She was building the kind of Community she had always longed for.

As this group came together, something within her began to reawaken. She started to rediscover her passions and rebuild her sense of self. She was realigning her life with her own vision, surrounding herself with people who felt like home and stepping into the woman she was always meant to be.

Still, I worried. I masked it the best I could, but inside, I was scared. I missed the spark in her eyes. I just wanted to see her light up again.

Around the same time, I was planning to attend another year of the Summit of Greatness. I didn't have a personal goal set this time; I was going for her. I wanted Gianna to come with me, to see if this Community of inspiration might help reignite her inner flame. After everything—the shift in her lost friendships, the emotional toll, and then losing her dream internship due to COVID—she needed something to help her rise again. We all did. But especially her.

I showed up to that year's Summit a bit of a basket case. Thankfully, the Michelles were with me, knowing how much I wanted this weekend to spark something in Gianna. I didn't want to push or guide her. I just wanted her to experience what I had: a room full of driven, kind, inspiring people all chasing growth. My extended Summit Squad was also behind me in the background helping in any way they could.

The year prior, I had met a young woman at the event named Olimpia—spunky, full of life, about Gianna's age. She stood out because there weren't many teens or young adults there. I talked to her mom at one of the social events and told her, "It's so incredible you brought your daughter. I hope to do the same someday."

I remember calling Gianna after that and saying, "G, you have to come to Summit next year. You would love this." I could feel the excitement in myself just imagining it. So when the dates were announced, I told her: "You're coming and I bought our tickets!"

And what happened next was nothing short of amazing.

The Michelles, Gianna, and I boarded our flight to Columbus, Ohio, where Summit was taking place at that time. My husband, who wasn't one for big events like this, had to trust me—like he always did—that this was the right move for her. At that point, we were both cheering for any positive momentum she could gain. I remember feeling hopeful as soon as we arrived. And just as I had dreamed, the spark came back. Almost immediately, Gianna began connecting with others—in line, before we even stepped inside.

It felt like there were a few more students that year—maybe other parents were inspired by sweet Olimpia, too. Gianna quickly found her own "Summit Squad." I sat back with the Michelles, my heart swelling with joy and love as I watched everything I'd been hoping for unfold in front of me.

The Community, the inspiration, the accountability—all of it was there. People with different dreams, different backgrounds from all over the world, all gathered in one room to be challenged, supported, and lifted up. That weekend brought Gianna and me closer. We stopped everything else and just focused. We gained insights from the speakers, opened up to each other, and leaned into the vulnerability we usually avoid in the day-to-day. There was no walking away. There was only showing up—for each other and for ourselves.

And yes—Gianna and Olimpia finally met. Just as I'd imagined, they clicked. Each became part of the other's Summit circle.

But the highlight? On the final night, at the closing social hour, I watched Gianna, surrounded by her new friends, her spark fully reignited. In a crowded room with music thumping and people cheering, there she was in the center of a dance circle, smiling, glowing, dancing. A new version of her was unfolding. The confident, bold, radiant Gianna was back. I turned to the Michelles, tears in my eyes, and whispered, "She's back."

And then—because of course she would—she ended up on stage dancing with Wyclef Jean, Lewis Howes, and Olimpia. That night is one we will never forget.

It was this Community that helped fuel her fire. She returned the following year, still connected to her friends and accountability partners from before, expanding her network and her light.

Gianna and I had always shared a strong bond, but after that transformational weekend at the Summit, something shifted between us. We began having deeper, more honest conversations—not just about where she was emotionally, but about what it means to grow, to struggle, and to rise again. I, too, learned I needed to let her be the person she wanted to become. As parents we spend many years wanting to control, support, and guide our children in the right direction, and I needed to let her push toward her path as an adult. One of the things we talked about often was titanium; the word itself had become a symbol between us. Titanium is lightweight, incredibly strong, and resistant to corrosion. It bends, but it doesn't break. It became a perfect metaphor for the kind of strength we both needed to embrace—resilient, quiet, enduring.

Even though it had always been part of our family mantra, the word titanium started showing up in our conversations more and more. It was no longer just about her healing; it was about mine, too. In helping her rekindle her fire, I was rediscovering things I loved to do, listening to inspiring individuals, pulling what I could from them, and getting back into journaling, something I hadn't done since high school. We talked about the importance of staying grounded in who we are, even when life throws curveballs. And most importantly, we reopened the door to honest, open communication. That space allowed us to connect not only as mother and daughter, but as two women growing through life together.

A few months later, Gianna and I decided to make this bond permanent. We took a little road trip to L.A., just the two of us. Along the way, we visited some family and a tattoo artist we'd followed for some time. We commemorated our trip and sealed our relationship with matching titanium tattoos on our inner wrists. It wasn't just ink. It was a reminder in the moment of the strength we have built as strong women tackling our own challenges in life—a bond and a daily reminder that we are titanium, a symbol of every moment we felt lost but kept going anyway. A promise to ourselves and each other that no matter what life throws at us, we carry an unshakable strength.

Now, when the days are heavy or the path feels uncertain, we look down and remember: we've already overcome so much. We've bent, but we've never broken. And with titanium in our blood and in our hearts, we're not done growing yet.

Life is full of messy parts—moments wrapped in self-doubt, insecurity, comparison, and overthinking. But what if our imperfections aren't flaws to fix or hide? What if they are invitations—calling us toward something deeper, something more real?

Growth rarely happens in the quiet, easy moments. Instead, it shows up in the chaos—in the unraveling, the uncertainty, the parts that challenge who we think we are. And when we choose to be open—to speak our truth, to let others in, and to lean into the strength of Community—the mess begins to transform. It no longer defines us by pain alone but by purpose.

There's wisdom waiting in the mess; if we're brave enough to stop running, to stay present, and to walk through it… together.

Josh's Soccer Photos

Gianna and Olympia at Summit
with the Mother/Daughter crew

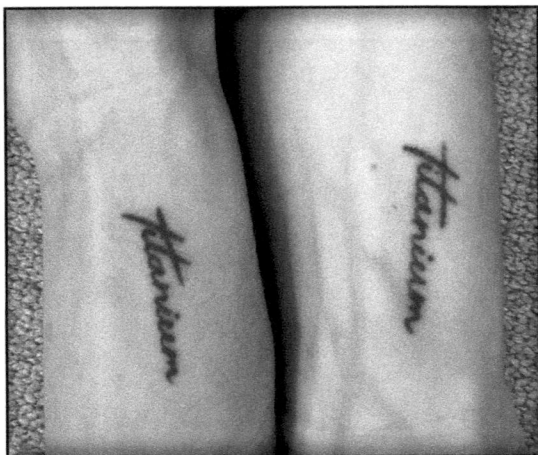

Tattoos

Group Summit Photo

Lori and sister, Lisa, adults

Family Photo

CHAPTER 9

FINDING YOUR OWN TITANIUM STRENGTH

There are moments in life when someone faces the unimaginable, and instead of shattering, they bend with a grace that defies the weight they carry. It's not always in the headlines or viral videos. Sometimes, it's in the quiet courage of a single mother holding her world together after an exhausting day. It's in the friend who shows up smiling while silently fighting their own storm. It's in the co-worker or loved one battling illness or grief, choosing day by day to keep going. That is the essence of Titanium Strength. It doesn't demand attention or applause.

It endures in silence, shines in resilience, and proves that the greatest strength is often found in the gentlest perseverance in life's most trying moments. Building *Titanium Strength* is about becoming resilient through it all. It's a combination of *Mental Fortitude*, *Emotional Flexibility*, and the unwavering *support of true Community* that creates real, lasting strength.

As I've shared throughout these pages, my story has been a mosaic of moments: growing up as the youngest, navigating self-doubt and growing confidence, pouring my heart into others, building deep friendships, opening myself to vulnerability, and walking through tragedy, trauma, love, and loss. These are *my* chapters, but the themes are universal. The scenes and circumstances may differ, but the undercurrent is the same: The human experience is messy, painful, beautiful, and brave.

This isn't just my look back. It's an invitation for you to take your own—to pause, reflect, and see your journey from the outside looking in. Because when we step back, we realize something powerful: We've already overcome so much. And if we choose to be honest, open, and willing to grow, we'll discover a truth that's been there all along: We are stronger than we ever believed. We are *titanium*.

While inner strength is crucial, no one thrives alone. I want to speak especially to those who may not have a large circle of friends or who struggle with social anxiety. I see you. I've felt that isolation at times, too. But here's the truth: Even the strongest among us need Community. We need connection—not always with crowds but with the *right* people. Thankfully, the world is becoming increasingly open to these conversations. Mental health, belonging, support— these are no longer whispered topics; they're front and center. So, if you've been waiting for permission to seek your people, consider this your invitation. Take the risk. Join the group. Say hello. The smallest step toward connection might lead you to your tribe, and your tribe will help remind you who you are when you forget.

After my dad passed, I watched something quietly powerful and unexpectedly beautiful begin to unfold. My mother, hollowed by grief and adjusting to a life she never imagined living alone, suddenly found herself surrounded by familiar faces from decades past—women she hadn't spoken to in years. They were childhood friends from grammar school; some she had only shared fleeting connections with, others she hadn't heard from in ages. But one by one, they showed up—not just with condolences, but with warm embraces, shared memories, and steady hands that helped hold her heart together.

It was as if time had folded in on itself, bringing these women back when she needed them most, like the universe was orchestrating a reunion of strength around her. They came without expectation, offering companionship, laughter, and the kind of support that only old friends can give. Slowly, almost imperceptibly, my mother began to move again. Like a dim light flickering back to life, her spirit started to stir.

These women didn't just comfort her; they sparked something within her she hadn't felt in a long time. It reminded me of a real-life *Stella Got Her Groove Back* moment, only more sacred and more grounded. My mom began taking small but brave steps: getting in the car and driving herself to the store, tackling everyday tasks she had long leaned on my dad to handle. She figured out how to fix things around the house—though every now and then, she'd still look up and call out to him in frustration or habit, hoping he might guide her somehow from wherever he was.

Nothing about it was easy. The grief still lingers like a shadow in the room, quietly present even on good days. But she keeps showing up. She keeps trying. And that—the determination to keep living, to keep moving forward even on the mornings when she didn't want to get out of bed—is Titanium Strength.

My sister and nephew have stayed close, always ready to help. But something within my mom has clearly shifted. The woman who once leaned so fully on her partner is now discovering her own strength, her own voice, her own sense of agency. Whether she knows it or not, she is becoming a quiet, living portrait of resilience, courage, and a deeply rooted kind of independence.

Taking the time to pause and truly reflect on moments like these—moments of quiet strength, unexpected support, and personal transformation—isn't just important, it's necessary. Life moves fast, and we often overlook the very things that shape us the most. But when we slow down long enough to notice the resilience we've built, the courage we've shown, and the ways we've grown, we start to see the outline of something extraordinary within ourselves. We begin to recognize our own Titanium Strength—the deep well of Mental Fortitude, Emotional Flexibility, and quiet courage built on Community Support that carries us forward when everything else feels uncertain.

That spirit deserves to be celebrated.

When I look at the Summit of Greatness Community I've been fortunate to be a part of, I see that Titanium Strength reflected in so many people. Over the years, I've witnessed individuals step into their truth, take bold risks, and evolve into more powerful versions of themselves. Watching their journeys unfold hasn't just been exciting; it's been soul-stirring. It reminded me that healing and growth are possible when you surround yourself with people who uplift, challenge, and walk beside you.

Communities like Brenden, DJ, Daya, Dez, Kim, the Michelles and Gianna didn't just attend Summit events; they leaned in fully. They embraced the discomfort of growth, turned inspiration into action, and redefined what success looked like for them. Some launched businesses, others mended relationships, and many simply decided to stop living small. They chose bravery over fear. And in doing so, they became reminders—to me and to others—that greatness isn't about perfection. It's about presence, persistence, and the willingness to keep showing up.

I could share story after story about this Community—the breakthroughs, the friendships, the tears, the triumphs—but at the end of the day, what matters most is this: you have that same power within you. Your Titanium Strength may not roar; it may whisper. But it's there. It's been with you all along, waiting for the moment you decide to believe in it and in yourself.

When I started writing this book, I didn't set out to change the world. I just hoped that maybe one person—just one—would feel seen, understood, and a little less alone. If even a small part of my journey sparked something inside you, gave you hope, or reminded you of your own strength, then sharing these pages has been more than worth it.

But I also want to say this clearly: These reflections are not a replacement for professional support. If you're carrying pain, trauma, or experiences that feel too heavy to process alone, please know that therapy, counseling, and healing communities are powerful and necessary tools. You don't have to navigate this journey in isolation. Seeking help is not weakness; it's wisdom. It's an act of self-respect and courage.

This book isn't a manual or a miracle. It's an invitation.

This is an invitation to pause. To reflect. To reconnect with the part of you that's already whole, already strong, already more than enough.

Because building Titanium Strength isn't about being unbreakable. It's about choosing to keep going through the losses, the doubts, the grief, and the growth. It's about honoring the battles you've faced and still finding the strength to rise again.

My hope is somewhere along the way, you've paused—maybe just for a moment—and felt something resonate. Maybe it's helped you notice your own resilience. Maybe it's reminded you of the quiet ways you've already been building your own *Titanium Strength*. This is about recognizing the strength that's already within you. Through reflection, through connection, and through every brave step you take, you are building a life that doesn't just survive the storms—but learns how to dance in the rain, rebuild in the aftermath, and rise again. Stronger. Softer. And more grounded in your truth.

Because resilience isn't just about making it through.

It's about rising with more heart, more wisdom, and a deeper belief in yourself than ever before.

ACKNOWLEDGMENTS

To my parents, my family, and childhood friends— thank you for being my first foundation of love, strength, and belonging.

To my husband and our incredible children—you are my heart, my why, and the greatest joy of my life.

To the friends and co-workers who have walked beside me through every season— your presence has brought light, growth, and unwavering support.

To the mentors I've learned from and grown up with along the way— your guidance helped shape my perspective, sharpen my purpose, and fuel my evolution.

And to the changemakers who inspire us to reach beyond our limits—thank you to Lewis Howes, the Michelles and my extended Summit of Greatness family. Your commitment to showing up, encouraging others, and believing in human potential has made a lasting impact on my life, and your growth keeps inspiring me to grow. You are proof that Community is everything.

ABOUT THE AUTHOR

Lori Barbarotto is a storyteller of strength, truth, and transformation. Born and raised in San Francisco, she has walked a path marked by both quiet adversity and unthinkable trauma—including the life-altering experience of being kidnapped as an adult. Yet through it all, Lori was unknowingly building something powerful that she would later come to call her Titanium Strength.

In this deeply personal debut, Lori shares the stories—some painful, some empowering—that slowly and silently forged her inner strength over the years. But it wasn't until she discovered the power of *Community* that she truly recognized what had been taking shape within her all along. That connection became the final piece—the awakening—that allowed her to see her resilience, claim her voice, and rise like a phoenix from the ashes of survival into a life of purpose.

This book is more than a memoir; it's an invitation. Lori's hope is that by sharing her journey, others will see pieces of themselves in her story—and realize they, too, are stronger than they know. Even in the darkest moments, Titanium Strength is already being built. You only have to believe it's there.

You can connect with Lori on Instagram @titaniumstrength2025.

www.ingramcontent.com/pod-product-compliance
Lightning Source LLC
Chambersburg PA
CBHW061601220326
41597CB00053B/1944